"It's the most exciting time
in history to be a dad."

– Professor Richard Fletcher

THE
FATHER
HOOD

Inspiration For The New Dad Generation

Luke Benedictus
Jeremy Macvean
Andrew McUtchen

CONTENTS

TFH

Shit just got real.

The origin story of *the-father-hood.com*: a new destination for modern dads.

Luke Benedictus

Father of Joe and Marc

Jeremy Macvean

Father of Amara, Nellie and Violet

Andrew McUtchen

Father of Indie, Isla and Neve, and friend of stepdaughter, Alyssa

IT ALL STARTED ON A BOAT WITH THOR AND JASON BOURNE . . . .

Andrew It all started on a boat with Thor and Jason Bourne. Through a bizarre twist of fate, I'd somehow ended up spending three days on a boat in Monaco with Chris Hemsworth and Matt Damon for work. It was on that boat that I had this 'dad moment', where things I had been thinking about for a long time sort of started to crystallise for me.

All we talked about was family and life strategy. How Matt Damon will never hire a nanny again because his kids were so traumatised by the loss of their first nanny. How Chris Hemsworth has decided that he's done with trying to structure having a family around his career, so he's now decided to structure a career around his family. Everyone was off the leash—there were no kids around—yet all we talked about was our lives as dads, and how foregrounded, how primary that role was in the way we manage our careers, structure our time and live our lives.

Yes, those guys have more money than we'll ever dream of. But they're still struggling with their own family dramas as dads. It made me realise what a universal thing this is. And then Jeremy sent me an email . . .

Jeremy That's right. That email shared my gut feeling that something was happening among dads. Through my work at Movember, it was clear to see that a lot of dads were struggling. Of course, mums have it really tough—this isn't a competition—but women generally have better social connections. They're often better at communicating, and they also have heaps of online options, like mummy blogs, social media and so on, to share and discuss their issues as mums.

I told Andrew that I wished there was something out there to help me as a dad, and writing those words helped me pin the idea down. I was able to see the need in black and white.

Luke

Andrew had flagged the idea of doing something in the dad space a while back on a plane trip. At the time, I thought it was a great idea, but I didn't have kids myself yet, so it didn't resonate with the same urgency. Still, it was a long-haul flight—we were both going to Rio for the Olympics—and we ended up getting pretty drunk. By the time we got off the plane, I'd accidentally given him a column in *Men's Health*, the magazine I was editor of, to write about the joys and horrors of fatherhood.

But the main thing I remember about that conversation was what I didn't actually remember.

About a month afterwards, I spoke to Andrew on the phone and asked how he was going. 'Pretty good,' he said. 'Although I'm going to hospital tomorrow to have that procedure I told you about on the plane.'

And I had no idea what he was talking about.

I came home and said to my wife, 'Andrew is going to hospital to have an operation! I don't know what's wrong with him! Maybe he's really sick? I'm such a bad friend! He's confided this big thing to me but I was too drunk to remember what it was! Maybe he's got cancer?'

Sarah said, 'What are you on about? He's probably just having a vasectomy—he's got three kids under three.' And she was right. Again.

TFH

Jeremy	What also helped to spark things was that Andrew and I have these kind of mirrored lives. We both have three daughters about the same age. We both have psychologist wives. We're both into music. We have mutual mates. So while we met through work, whenever we chatted we'd always talk about our families and lives.
Andrew	Because of all these crazy similarities, you and I could have these really open conversations. We'd created this safe and honest space over common ground. We could talk about all the joys of our families over a beer, but could also say, 'Having three small kids is really hard.' Or, 'This is bullshit! Who would sign on for this?' Or, 'I haven't slept since the Howard era. I hate my life!'
Jeremy	This was one of the things that inspired The Father Hood. We wanted to create a platform to share those types of stories and perspectives that we were having in our one-on-one chats.
Andrew	So we got together over a few pints and nutted out the details of what we wanted to create with *the-father-hood.com*: an online space to offer support, advice and inspiration for dads. Four months later, we were publishing our first post.
Luke	In which David Beckham explained that his secret dad-hack for getting his kids to eat more vegetables is to smuggle them into strawberry smoothies.
Jeremy	And that's the thing, we all go through so many common experiences as dads, just like this, but we tend to experience them in isolation. This is partly because men often lose connection with their mates when they become dads, but also because guys tend not to be so great at talking about these things either. If we can share those fatherhood experiences, hopefully people reading will feel, *OK, I'm not the only person going through this*. It'll make the challenges they face seem smaller and the opportunities seem brighter. There's no doubt fatherhood can prove a really demanding time in a man's life, but we felt that if we could create a platform to share this stuff, it would make this time so much easier to navigate.

Andrew Yes, I just don't think that men identify with each other as dads in the same way that women identify with each other as mums. What we'd love to encourage is for mates who are already in strong male groups and going through the same issues and challenges just to have the chat. You're all there, so the network already exists. You're just not lighting up that particular circuitry.

> **"All the stats show that dads are more actively involved in their kids' lives than ever before."**

Luke And we're at a point in history when men are more open to doing that. All the stats show that dads are more actively involved in their kids' lives than ever before. There's research to prove modern dads now spend three times as many hours with their kids each week than dads did back in the 1960s. This book is a celebration of that change.

Jeremy Yeah, the traditional concept of fatherhood has totally flipped on its head in one generation. For parents today, the rulebook is out. We're all making it up as we go, so we absolutely need to be bouncing ideas off each other.

Luke That generational shift really hit home to me when I was speaking to my father-in-law, who's a devoted family man, shortly before my first son was born. I was asking him about the birth of my wife, who's his oldest child, and my father-in-law revealed that he wasn't in the delivery room for her birth.

'So what was the story there?' I asked. 'Were you out of town for work or something?' 'No,' he said, 'I was at the cricket. It was Day Three of the Ashes at the MCG.'

Jeremy That shows how much things have changed.

TFH

Luke   Yeah, we no longer have eight-ball overs in test cricket either. But relationships have also changed massively. Andrew, do you remember that chat we had at the pub in The Rocks? That day you'd posted something very out of character on Facebook. Usually, you're pretty upbeat and gung-ho about everything. But you'd written this post that basically said: 'Shout out to all the mums and dads. Sometimes this parenting business is just so hard.'

By this stage, I'd just had my second son in the space of sixteen months. It was a crazy time at home and at work. Right then, I didn't want to be smacked between the eyes with the raw truth. I just wanted gentle reassurance that everything was going to be OK.

Andrew   You came up to me like, 'Mate, what the hell's all that about?' And what it was about was my wife had just gone back to full-time work and we had three small kids.

I'd always said to my wife that I wanted her to be able to have the career she was born for. Yes, I wanted us to have children, but not at the expense of her work. Our plan was that we were going to try and have it all.

> **"Traditional gender roles are changing so rapidly. But we're the first generation to have to figure out a way to make it work."**

But on the night I wrote that post, I was up in Sydney for work and my wife was down in Melbourne with three kids and she had to facilitate an event the next day for 1000 people. And it just wasn't working, because it doesn't work. It wasn't a sustainable situation.

Traditional gender roles are changing so rapidly. But we're the first generation to have to figure out a way to make it work. That's partly what The Father Hood is about—making sense of this brave new world, where the pillars of family life have completely shifted, but doing it together.

Jeremy	And the word 'together' is really important. Because this can't become a gender battle, that's not what it's about. It's about figuring it out together, as families.
Luke	Plus, the truth is, the three of us desperately need these solutions ourselves because we're all living it and flailing about trying to find that elusive balance. We've all got young kids, and we're constantly having these ridiculous three-way work phone calls that get interrupted mid-way by some slapstick disaster. Like my son falling down the stairs . . .
Andrew	Hang on a sec, fellas. My kid's eating dog food again.
Luke	Or doing a poo underneath the trampoline.
Jeremy	But we go into this with confidence that something important is happening because the response has been beyond anything we'd expected. And that's from both men and women. In fact, what's surprised us is the number of mums who have said, 'Yeah, we do actually need the role of dad to be a hero. He's got an important role and we need the spotlight shone on dads.' That's been a real eye-opener. To learn that people around dads are so aware that happier, more confident, more hands-on dads will lead to happier families. The Father Hood is equally a place for women to have a voice in the role of fathers. It's not just a dads' club.
Luke	Yes, and we've been humbled by the reaction. The feedback we've had from people is that this is a big issue, and not just for dads, but for men in general. Remember when we were outlining our plans over a coffee with Jonni, that meditation expert? At the end of our chat, he turned to us and said: 'So basically what you guys are going to do is to reset the trajectory of manhood for the future of humanity.'
Andrew	And we said: 'Well, yeah. Although we're still not exactly sure what we'll do in week two . . .'

TFH

LIFE TURNED UP TO 11

YOU ARE DAD ...

Short-order cook; nappy changer; writer and singer of songs; giver of backpats and shoulder massages; mixologist of baby bottles and after-work cocktails;

teller of stories,
tall and true;
giver of ridiculous
nicknames.
Lover. Fighter
for your family.
You are no parent's
assistant. You are
Dad. Hands on.
Always on. Hero.

"ACTIONS OBVIOUSLY SPEAK LOUDER THAN WORDS."

Mark Wahlberg

Father of Ella, Michael, Brendan and Grace

Actor / Producer / Businessman

INTERVIEW BY
Jenny Cooney / HFPA

I think the most important
thing about being a dad
is to be an example.
For me, that comes through
in my work ethic, the kind
of focus that I have, my faith,
what I have with my family,
as well as my profession
and the other businesses
that I'm involved with.

Mark Wahlberg

When it comes to your kids, you can preach one thing, but if you're doing another they're still seeing what you're doing. And actions obviously speak louder than words.

Of course they're going to choose what they're going to do in life, but I want them to work hard. It's funny, because only in America can you—in one generation—turn things around, but also—in another generation—lose everything. So I hope they're just motivated and inspired to do the right thing.

I don't force my kids to go to church with me, but I make sure that I'm going. No matter what's going on, I have to go. And I have to start my day reading and then in prayer. Hopefully, they'll see that those things work for me, and know that Dad became successful because he was willing to work harder than everybody else. And if I can give them that, then they're good.

"Hopefully they'll see that Dad became successful because he was willing to work harder than everybody else."

I still want to give my kids all the things I never had. They're always saying, 'Dad, this house is way too big, let's move into this other house.' I worked to make sure that I could give them all the things that I thought they would want— things that I wanted when I was younger. But the most important things are having family, having your faith and having each other.

XOXOXOXOXOXOXOXOXOXOXOXOXOXOXOXOX
XOXOXOXOXOXOXOXOXOXOXOXOXOXOXOXOXO
XOXOXOXOXOXOXOXOXOXOXOXOXOXOXOXOX
XOXOXOXOXOXOXOXOXOXOXOXOXOXOXOXOXO
XOXOXOXOXOXOXOXOXOXOXOXOXOXOXOXOX
XOXOXOXOXOXOXOXOXOXOXOXOXOXOXOXOXO
XOXOXOXOXOXOXOXOXOXOXOXOXOXOXOXOX
XOXOXOXOXOXOXOXOXOXOXOXOXOXOXOXOXO
XOXOXOXOXOXOXOXOXOXOXOXOXOXOXOXOX
XOXOXOXOXOXOXOXOXOXOXOXOXOXOXOXOXO
XOXOXOXOXOXOXOXOXOXOXOXOXOXOXOXOX
XOXOXOXOXOXOXOXOXOXOXOXOXOXOXOXOXO
XOXOXOXOXOXOXOXOXOXOXOXOXOXOXOXOX
XOXOXOXOXOXOXOXOXOXOXOXOXOXOXOXOXO
XOXOXOXOXOXOXOXOXOXOXOXOXOXOXOXOX
XOXOXOXOXOXOXOXOXOXOXOXOXOXOXOXOXO
XOXOXOXOXOXOXOXOXOXOXOXOXOXOXOXOX
XOXOXOXOXOXOXOXOXOXOXOXOXOXOXOXOXO
XOXOXOXOXOXOXOXOXOXOXOXOXOXOXOXOX
XOXOXOXOXOXOXOXOXOXOXOXOXOXOXOXOXO
XOXOXOXOXOXOXOXOXOXOXOXOXOXOXOXOX
XOXOXOXOXOXOXOXOXOXOXOXOXOXOXOXOXO
XOXOXOXOXOXOXOXOXOXOXOXOXOXOXOXOX
XOXOXOXOXOXOXOXOXOXOXOXOXOXOXOXOXO
XOXOXOXOXOXOXOXOXOXOXOXOXOXOXOXOX
XOXOXOXOXOXOXOXOXOXOXOXOXOXOXOXOXO
XOXOXOXOXOXOXOXOXOXOXOXOXOXOXOXOX
XOXOXOXOXOXOXOXOXOXOXOXOXOXOXOXOXO
XOXOXOXOXOXOXOX
XOXOXOXOXOXOXO
XOXOXOXOXOXOXOX
XOXOXOXOXOXOXO
XOXOXOXOXOXOXOX

3120 – The combined number of kisses (1456) and cuddles (1664) you'll receive from your child before they turn four.

A REVOLUTION OF THE DEEPEST KIND

Steve Biddulph

Father and grandfather

Retired psychologist / Bestselling author of *Raising Boys* and *The New Manhood*

At the age of seventy-four, my father
was diagnosed with cancer of the liver.
Within twelve weeks he was dead.
With the help of modern pain control,
we made good use of the time—
talking, hanging out, getting ready.
Which isn't to say there weren't times
of racking sorrow, or confusion and
pain, but, for the most part, it was
a peaceful dying.

Shortly before the morphine
began to carry him beyond reach,
my father recounted, out of the
blue, an incident from my early life.
What he told me, haltingly, seemed
to embody the struggle men have
had to wage in order to be allowed
to fully experience fatherhood.
Days after my birth in 1953, when
we had returned from hospital
to the grimy Yorkshire town where
we lived, my father took me out
in the pram, perhaps to give my
mother some peace. He bundled
me up and set off towards the town
centre—I imagine his choice of route
involved some element of pride,
but perhaps it just offered more
shelter from the icy winds.

As he entered the high street,
he noticed passersby reacting oddly.
Some were openly scornful; some
looked amused. But the final straw
came when a group of children,
unoccupied, began to follow along
and taunt him.

'What were they saying?' I asked.
He remembered the words exactly;
it was a kind of chant. 'Your dad's
your mum,' he said, and his voice
slipped back into the north country
vowels the kids used all those years
ago. In the end, the whole thing
had been too much for him—he was
a shy man at the best of times—and
he turned off down a side street,
and went quickly home.

TFH

As my father closed his eyes to rest, I pictured the vulnerable-looking young man I had seen in family photos colliding headlong with the tight role definitions of 1950s working-class England. He was a 'new man' fifty years before his time. And the thought occurred to me that he could hardly have been unique in this. How many millions of young fathers, animated with the joy of new fatherhood and the instinctive urge to tenderness, had, through social pressures, clamped down on their feelings? How many, even worse, had turned them into harshness and violence?

That my father had chosen to tell this story from the beginning of my life at the end of his own seemed loaded with meaning. He had read my books on parenthood. He had sat with gruff pride at the back of my lectures on healing the rifts between fathers and sons. He could not have failed to take some of this personally; he and I had not always been on good terms, and our peaceful closeness was only a recent and hard-won possession.

What he was trying to tell me was hardly rocket science: it was his way of saying, 'I tried, son.' But my father more than tried; he brought our family to Australia against all the odds, he remained an affectionate, playful, sacrificing parent in a turbulent age. He wasn't all I wanted, but what father ever was?

But this all went beyond the personal. He was a trade unionist, as his own father had been. He was attuned to injustice and the need to fight for what you believe. We don't blink today at a father pushing a pram, though it's still new enough to be heartwarming. It sounds trivial, but what it represents is a revolution of the deepest kind. Involved, hands-on fatherhood was almost crushed out of existence in the industrial era, but it fought back. Fatherly love has survived.

"We're not just expected to pay for things, earn the money and be the disciplinarian. I think we've got more permission now to be emotionally involved."

Steve Biddulph

"Involved, hands-on fatherhood was almost crushed out of existence in the industrial era, but it fought back. Fatherly love has survived."

I would like to be able to say that the crushing of fatherhood is a thing of the past. But today's men are still being riven from their children. It is not jeering street urchins so much as a political and economic climate that drives longer working hours and devalues both mothers and fathers in their primary role, while claiming to be family-friendly.

Families need a socially supportive context. The government still presides over policies that see human beings primarily as economic units. The government drags its feet on decent paternity and maternity leave, would prefer single parents working on checkouts rather than spending time with their toddlers at home. I fear there will be a new generation of young men and women who feel estranged from their parents if we do not turn this situation around. The Australian father of today still has a battle on his hands to stay close to his children, but the signs are good. A father's heart isn't easily silenced.

TFH

Your legacy starts now.

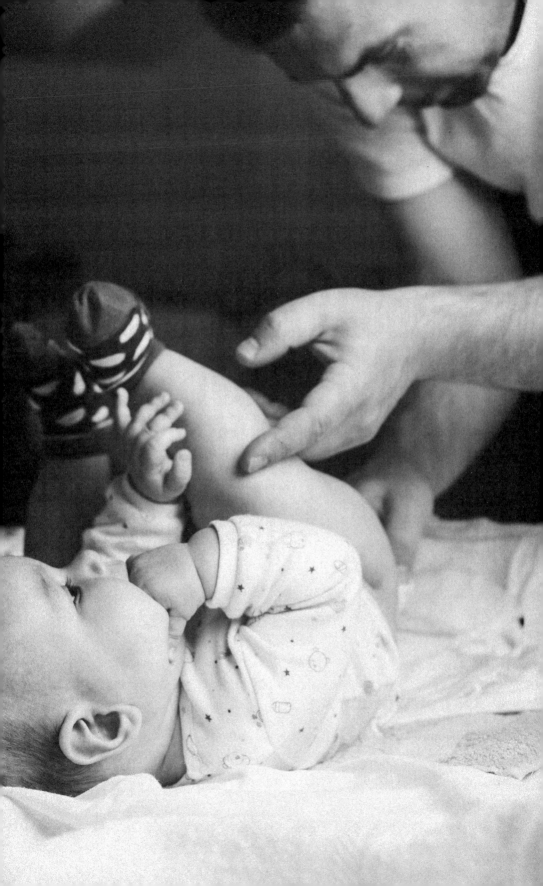

"THERE'S SOMETHING SUPER-WONDERFUL ABOUT DATING AND FALLING IN LOVE WITH A WOMAN WHO HAS A KID."

Osher Günsberg

Stepfather of Georgia

TV presenter

Being a stepdad is not without its challenges for all of us, because it's a new family unit for everyone to get used to. But I was unfazed by it. I met Audrey when I'd just turned forty, and the reality of being a single man in your forties is that you're going to date women with children. And I would recommend it. Highly.

There's something super-wonderful about dating and falling in love with a woman who has a kid; it's a different energy. The thing I found about Audrey straight away was that she just had her shit together 'cause there was no time to mess around. She was a single mum raising Georgia alone, and she just had it together because she had to. And I was thrilled.

The advice I'd give anyone becoming a stepdad for the first time is to understand that there is an existing relationship that you are now allowed to become a part of, and that's the relationship between the mum and her kid (or kids). And that will always be, and has to be, the priority. Always understand that you will never be number one. It's not about you—that's the thing. It's not about you anymore. And having that humility brings extraordinary opportunity. It can be hard at first, but that's okay.

Becoming a stepdad is like you're pulling onto the highway, my friend. It's not like when you have a baby and you're just getting up to a jogging pace, then you get up to a sprint and then you're running a marathon. You don't have that slow curve of getting used to the other things in your life dissipating and this being the priority; everything changes, man. And it's worth it. You become more of a man because of it. That's not to say the gear change isn't a shock, but it is an opportunity to man up.

You have to make it okay for your partner to choose the kid over you every single time, because you're a grown man and you can look after yourself. There's a child in the situation, with questions and opinions and emotions, who needs to be considered and taken care of. That absolutely has to be the priority. Suck it up.

TFH

You also have to be super-aware of how you can affect the relationship between your partner and her child or children. There's no point enriching your life by having a relationship with someone if you destroy another in the process. No! The only reason that you would want to be with this person is to make sure that those lives, everybody's lives, are lifted up. So you're not just enriching the life of the other person in the relationship. One plus one equals three, if you do it right.

I think what I didn't really expect about becoming a stepdad is how much things changed from one day to the next. One day, Georgia was my girlfriend's kid, who I hung out with and played *Dance Revolution Extreme* with on the Wii. The next, I felt like I'd do anything to save her life! Even if that meant pushing her out of the way of a train and me getting killed, I would do it.

It was like this switch got flicked in the back of my head and that was it. It's never changed since then. Boom! Locked in.

I've heard mates describe this happening sometimes in the first hours or days after their baby is born. It took a little longer for me because, obviously, Georgia is quite a grown-up kid. She was ten when I met her, but it didn't take long. It was only a couple of months of us hanging out. And it's just brought everything into utterly sharp focus. I'm really grateful for her.

Are there any key do's and don'ts to being a stepdad? The number one don't is don't try to be their dad. Just be a person of integrity in that child's life. Be a person who is able to show the child what a loving and caring relationship can be like. That'll be the greatest gift you can give to them. They will call the shots of the depth of the relationship you have with them. You might just be the person that drives them around. That's okay. You might be the person they ask for advice. You might be the person they don't want to hear a thing from. That's okay.

The greatest advice given to me about being a stepfather, or taking on a father role, is that, yeah, they might ignore you. But the most important thing is that you're there for them to ignore. You've just gotta be there. Just. Be. There. As long as you show that you're there and that you love their mum, and you love and care for them, down the track that will pay off.

What's the secret to a lasting marriage? (Full disclosure: this is my second time around.) Communication is important. Validation is important. Making sure that you are man enough to not let your ego jump in the way. Admitting when you're at fault and taking responsibility. Being super-accountable.

You may have brought things from your previous relationship into this one. And it may be habitual, like when you rent a European car for a weekend when you're in another city and you keep turning the indicator on when you're trying to change the windshield wiper, or the other way around. Like you don't mean to do it, it's just a reaction. And you need to go, 'Oh, that's a thing that doesn't belong here. Sorry. I'm gonna try and work on that. I know I shouldn't do that.' Do everything you can to try and change that, and show her that you're trying to change that.

The relationship is going to change under your feet, and that is fine. Those first six or nine months are blissful and wonderful, and then it can get down to times when it seems like the only conversations you seem to have are about bills and logistics about moving kids around.

It's also important to remember a relationship takes work. You don't just accidentally have a great marriage. You make critical decisions, every hour of every day. You make choices every hour and every day that take you towards that great marriage. And that's what a great relationship takes. It takes work.

It's like anything; you can't just set it and forget it or it will perish. It will perish like a pot plant that you bought one weekend when you thought, *I'm gonna have an indoor garden!* And what you're doing now is you've got a bunch of empty pots stacked on top of each other on the balcony because they all died. No, you've got to work on your marriage every day. But it's worth it.

TFH

True fatherhood goes way beyond human biology. As Obama points out so eloquently here, the basic ability to have a child is not what makes you a man.

These words were spoken during a fiery speech at a Chicago church in 2008, where he railed against the epidemic of fatherless families and called on men to embrace their responsibilities. The subtext of this address was deeply personal: Obama's own father abandoned the family when he was a toddler.

In his personal life, Obama vowed to break the cycle of the absent father, and becoming the leader of the free world wasn't going to stop him. Once established in the White House, Obama and his wife, Michelle, made the decision to prioritise family dinners, and consequently he insisted on sitting down for dinner with his wife and daughters at six-thirty every night. He only conceded to miss this a maximum of twice a week.

This was a big call for a president, and not without its repercussions. It limited Obama's availability to his aides, his fundraising trips, his outreach to Congress and more.

Yet Obama's decision was founded on his unshakable belief in the importance of family.

It was a sentiment that he expanded on in a 2013 speech in Virginia, where he claimed that no job is more important than being a good dad. And when addressing the graduating class at Morehouse College that same year, Obama reasoned that on his deathbed he wouldn't be pondering his policies or even the Nobel Peace Prize that he won, he'd be thinking of moments shared with his daughters and his wife. Long walks, lazy afternoons and evenings shared together around the dinner table. His legacy will revolve around how he measured up in the eyes of his family. And, in his words, 'Whether I did right by all of them.'

TFH

Bears
Lizards
Otters
Monkeys
Hamsters
Snakes
Meerkats
Lions

All of these creatures have been known to eat their young.

So don't be quite so hard on yourself when you yell at your kid.

STRONGER. WISER. CALMER.

Alex Laguna's marriage break-up tore his life apart. But through it, he learned the coping tactics to become a better dad.

The morning it happened, Alex hadn't the slightest inkling that life as he knew it was about to end. Divorce caught him totally off-guard.

He was heading off to work when his wife stopped him: 'She just said, "I don't love you anymore. I don't want to be with you anymore",' he recalls. 'I bloody nearly fell over.'

The couple had two children: a three-year-old son and a four-year-old daughter. The most crushing part of the break-up was that Alex would no longer be able to live with his kids.

Alex Laguna

'To be honest, it completely fucked me,'
he says. 'I had this concept of what my
family was and what it was going to be.
Having that stripped away from me
and not being able to see my kids . . .
that was just so heavy to manage.'

Forced to move out, Alex rented a
nearby house to stay as close to his kids
as possible. But confronting the stark
reality of this new life very nearly broke
him: 'I woke up one day in this new house
with no furniture on a foam mattress
in a sleeping bag,' he says. 'I was ready
to take my bootlaces out and find the
closest rafter.'

'The way I felt then would probably not be uncommon for men going through divorce and separation. You're completely undone. The magnitude of what your life looks like at that moment is horrific.'

Eight years on, Alex has managed to rebuild his life. Happily remarried, he's had three more kids while also launching a successful business. His company, Laguna Lighting, provides the lighting design for TV shows like *MasterChef*. He has also founded a website that provides support, information and resources for dads: *BetterDads.com*.

"There was this big prize at stake, and that was being able to see my children. They were the most important people."

It's a comeback of Rocky Balboa proportions, but it didn't happen by chance. Turning things around involved hours of self-work and reflection propelled by the determination to manage the situation correctly for the sake of his kids. Along the way, Alex discovered certain tactics that he now credits with helping him to cope, recover and ultimately bounce back stronger.

'I still screw up as much as anyone,' he admits. 'I still have to focus on all these things daily. It's not a case of do something once and you're suddenly this new guy. But the five tips on the next few pages are some of the tactics that helped get me through it.'

TFH

ALEX'S TOP FIVE TACTICS FOR COPING WITH LIFE WHEN THINGS GET MESSY.

1 TALK TO SOMEONE

'When my wife left me, my old man actually told me to go and see a counsellor. Initially, I was really pissed off at him for saying that because I was still so angry. At that point I felt it was all my ex-wife's fault—you left me, you left the relationship, you broke the family. My attitude was really quite childish, and ultimately not very helpful.

My dad said to me, 'Listen, if you don't go to a counsellor, you'll end up in the same situation, the same scenario. You need to talk to someone about why this has happened. So in the end, I did go. And it was the best thing that I've ever done. It was completely life-changing.

The interesting thing was that I went in and started talking about my relationship with this woman. But then, just naturally, I started looking at all these other elements in my life. Why was I the person that I was? What was I was really like? Why do I do the things that I do?

Exploring those things enabled me to have some empathy for my ex-wife. It helped me to understand that she was struggling with her own things. That it must have been hard to break up the family for her, too. That it wasn't making her happy to do this. And so that took the steam out of the situation.

Talking to the counsellor helped me to get rid of the anger and the blame. When you're always blaming someone, it means you think everything is always someone else's fault. That's not the way to move forward.

Look, there were times after seeing that counsellor that I almost crawled out of there, broken. But afterwards I felt so good for it.

2 KEEP YOUR EYES ON THE PRIZE

My parents divorced when I was about nine years old and it was really messy. I think that made me hypersensitive about wanting to look after my kids throughout my divorce. My main focus became making sure they were okay, and that what they had to deal with was as smooth as possible. There was this big prize at stake, and that was being able to see my children. They were the most important people.

My ex-wife and I were in a situation that could escalate like . . . you have no idea how fast. It could just blow up whether in discussions or text messages! It was still difficult speaking with her, but my aim was to always try and stay as calm as possible. So I learned to not send that text message or reply to that email. I just tried to stay cool.

To do that, I had to really work on keeping my ego in check, because my ego is the thing that would have got me into huge strife earlier on. I learned that I didn't always have to win every argument. I learned that instead of disagreeing with my ex-wife, I could say: 'No, you're right, that's a great idea, let's do that.' She'd be swinging at me and all of a sudden it's like, hang on! There's no one there to swing at.

Often, arguments come down to pride and ego. There is no gain. So I just focused on my kids, and on trying to stay out of court and on making life as calm as possible between my ex and me. Because I also knew that if my kids were at her house and she's all fired up, well that's not a good environment for them. And that's why I never bring problems with my ex-wife home to my kids. Ever.'

Alex Laguna

3 USE EXERCISE TO CLEAR YOUR HEAD

Straight after the split, I got so sick of thinking about my divorce. It was always on my mind. I needed to clear my head, so I started going for walks to get some fresh air in my lungs. That was really helpful.

Then I said to myself that every time that I think about my divorce, I'm going to drop and do twenty push-ups straight away. So I ended up doing hundreds of them every day. Each time I'd get a little shot of endorphins, and it'd make me feel good, and all of a sudden I felt stronger. Things just grew from there. Soon I was running, and doing push-ups and chin-ups everywhere.

Exercise was unbelievably helpful for me. It really played a huge role. I was a single guy, so getting fitter helped me to feel better about myself and become more confident, even though I was still a bit beaten. Exercise made a huge difference. I can't recommend it highly enough.

"Often arguments come down to pride and ego. There is no gain."

4 GIVE YOURSELF SOME MENTAL SPACE

Taking some time for yourself every day is a really good idea. If you can stop for five minutes, close your eyes, take a few deep breaths and just try and let go of some of the pressure that you're holding on to, that can be really helpful when you're dealing with a lot of conflict and trying to remain calm.

You know what it's like; from the moment you wake up, your mind's racing. From dealing with everything at home to the kids, work, money . . . It never stops. Ever.

Meditation might be too far-fetched for some people, but I did a weekend course of transcendental meditation (TM) with this guy called Tim Brown in Sydney. What meditation did was give me the ability to calm everything down. It gets rid of all those layers of constant thought that pile pressure on you. All of a sudden you're not thinking about yourself and all those problems that stress you out so much.

The other thing meditation gave me was a greater ability to listen to other people. It helped me to empathise more with what they were going through, because it gave me the mental space to be able to do that. It really helped.

5 WORK ON YOUR SELF-AWARENESS

Self-awareness is probably the biggest one. With my first marriage, I think I just lost sight of my relationship. I was working so hard trying to build a business and stay employed in the film industry, which is a really tough field. I'm not sure if I was focused on work too much. You never know. But what I have learned is that I need to be more self-aware.

Now, with my wife, I try to think more about what I'm really like in my relationship. I think about my partner more. And I probably talk more openly and honestly when I'm struggling with things.

I don't always like being open. It's not easy for men, is it? It's this huge challenge for us and I can still struggle with it. But every time that I have shared my thoughts with my wife when I've felt stressed, I've felt this huge relief.

Self-awareness extends to being a dad, too. I'm my kids' role model and I've learned that it's my actions that they'll take on, not what I say. So I have to behave a certain way all the time. It's really important that you remember what you are and what you're like, even when your kids aren't around. Because ultimately, that's who you really are.

YOU'RE NOT MUM'S ASSISTANT

HOW A MOMENT BECAME A MOVEMENT

When Donte Palmer headed to a restaurant bathroom in Jacksonville, Florida, to change his son's nappy, he didn't know he was about to start a global movement. But an Instagram pic showing him being forced to squat down in the toilets to change his baby highlighted a pressing issue. As Donte explained in his original message:

"This is a serious post! What's the deal with not having changing tables in men's bathrooms as if we don't exist! #FLM #fatherslivesmatter clearly we do this often because look how comfortable my son is. It's routine to him! Let's fix this problem!"

Overnight, that post went viral. People around the world voiced their support and started sending in photos of their own similar experiences. The result was #squatforchange, a global campaign to raise awareness about the lack of changing facilities for dads.

The impact of Donte's post highlights the global zeitgeist of the hands-on dad. In 2019, fathers are now more actively involved in their children's lives than ever before. But that change isn't always reflected by prevailing attitudes and facilities. Luckily, men like Donte are tackling that challenge head-on.

Here, he recalls how one random moment evolved into a movement for modern dads.

DONTE'S STORY

It was a Saturday night and I was with my family in a local restaurant, the Texas Roadhouse, when Liam, my one-year-old, started crying.

If you're a parent and your baby starts crying, you know that it's always one of three things: they're either tired, hungry or they have a wet diaper. In this case, I found out it was pretty much all of the three.

So I went to the men's restroom with the baby, and Isaiah, my oldest son, came to help me. There was no changing table and, honestly, I wasn't very surprised. So I got into what I call my 'perfect man squat' with my back against the wall, and I began to change Liam's diaper across my thighs. It was nothing out of the ordinary.

Isaiah handed me the diaper and the wipes and then, when I was putting the diaper on, he pulled the phone out and just started snapping some pictures. And that was all there was to it. The picture wasn't even posted that day.

Two weeks later, I was at home watching the game and going through the phone, kind of bored. I came across that picture, thought it was interesting and decided to post it on social media to get some reactions from family and friends.

The next morning, my wife texted me: *Hey, check your phone.* When I picked it up, there were literally 1000 plus notifications on Facebook and Instagram. My phone was ringing. Reporters were messaging me, calling me.

From that moment on, it has not stopped.

To me, it's really amazing how one non-partisan issue can bring a lot of people together as parents, regardless of background, regardless of culture, regardless of sexual orientation.

We had an outpouring of positive messages. Jessica Alba emailed me directly on Instagram and said she supported my campaign and that she wanted to give us free diapers for life.

Donte Palmer

"Why did that picture go viral? Honestly, I think it's deeper than changing tables. What it shows is that men are now willing to be active parents."

We had people reaching out from across the world. Parents from Australia, South Africa, Brazil and Korea. We had people from The Gambia in West Africa saying, 'Hey, we don't even have toilets, but we still stand and support your movement.' And I was like, wow!

Why did that picture go viral? Honestly, I think it's deeper than changing tables. What it shows is that men are now willing to be active parents. And I don't know if that was really the case twenty years ago.

It shows a change in the narrative by saying the mothers aren't the only caretakers anymore, and that men—strong men with strong attitudes or strong personalities— can also be sensitive and say, 'Hey, we're here to really support and take care of our kids.'

I love changing my kid's diapers because that's a time when I'm looking at him eye to eye and it's meaningful. Right there, he can feel in his heart that his daddy is here and he cares for him.

When you're an active parent, your child knows: 'I can come to this man for anything, cause he cares for me, he doesn't judge me and if I have any problems, he's the first person I would go to, because I know damn well he'll be there to protect me.'

TFH

43

The percentage of UK fathers who'd <u>never</u> changed a nappy.

1982

63

The percentage of UK fathers who'd <u>never</u> changed a nappy.

%

2000

"WHAT IS IT THAT MAKES YOU HAPPY IN LIFE?"

Ben Stiller

Father of Ella and Quinlin

Actor / Producer / Director

INTERVIEW BY
Jenny Cooney / HFPA

Success can be measured in different ways. I think, for me over the years, it's changed. For a long time, I just loved doing what I do, and I focused on that without thinking about how that would relate to the rest of my life.

Ben Stiller

Then, as I got older and I had kids, I started to see how 'success' can also take you away from your personal relationships. Because when you're working all the time, and if you're devoting yourself to that, you have to figure out a way to balance it.

For me, that sort of evolved into figuring out what was going to make me happy and how I'm going to feel good as a parent. And sometimes that means not being able to do everything you want to do professionally.

That's made me a lot happier as a person. For me, my relationship with my kids is something I get a lot of happiness out of.

There's success commercially or professionally or artistically—those are all different things even within those categories. And then there's just, what is it that makes you happy in life?

"As I got older and I had kids, I started to see how that 'success' can also take you away from your personal relationships."

DROP THE ANCHOR

"When you are childless your identity is a fiction that can, necessarily, be rewritten."

– Will Self

Your freewheeling life may be over, but that's not necessarily a bad thing.

You're in the airport departure lounge when she catches your eye: the brown-haired woman in the tight sweater. She's so beautiful it makes you inwardly wince. When she returns your gaze with a sidelong smile, you strike up a conversation . . . Long story short, you hit it off, fall in love and end up moving around the world to her hometown of Rio where (spoiler alert!) you live happily ever after.

Now, if you don't have children, this scenario, while far-fetched, is not totally beyond the realms of possibility. When you've got kids, on the other hand, it's out of the question (or at least constitutes very shabby behaviour).

What Self is really saying here is that parenthood solidifies your existence. Suddenly, you're no longer a fictional character who can pursue the next spur-of-the-moment adventure. You can't simply reinvent your universe every time some Brazilian sex-bomb falls for your manifold charms.

There's no denying that fatherhood will curtail your freedom, but that's because what it really involves is the laying down of roots. You now have a duty to provide stability for your dependents. You have to forge routines, build traditions and make sure your kids feel safe and secure.

Don't mourn your previous existence. Sure, you've dropped the anchor on your life for the moment, but only because you're in a good place. There's no point in drifting away from here—especially when your shipmates are your favourite people in the world.

TFH

72% of new dads find their relationship is stronger after having kids.

TFH

THE LIFE OF A SINGLE DAD

Ben Dillon-Smith split with his partner when his son, Jethro, was five.

After moving out of the family home, he managed to get joint-custody of his son, and so began his new life as a single dad.

It hasn't always proved an easy transition, as Ben readily admits. Yet four years on, he's learned some valuable things about fatherhood, relationships and mental health. He writes about his experiences on his blog *thesingledadjourney.com*. 'You'll make lots of mistakes, but you're still their dad,' Ben says. 'And that can never be taken away from you.'

Read on as he shares some of his biggest learnings.

TFH

1 DROP-OFF DAY IS A NIGHTMARE

I fucking hate Wednesdays. I hate them because that's the day my son leaves to go back to his mum.

When you become a dad, you just take for granted that you wake up and your children are going to be there. Forget the finances or the property. Coming to terms with the realisation that there are now restrictions around when you can and can't see your children—that's the single hardest thing to deal with. It hurts.

I always notice a definite dip in my mood on Wednesdays. In fact, I can feel it building up the day before, knowing that the next morning I'm going to have to give Jethro back. Sometimes I even notice that I get a little bit short with him on Wednesday morning. I suppose it's the pressure of knowing what's going to happen.

How did I learn to manage Wednesdays? Partly, they just get easier with time, but you also have to be aware of the problem and be ready for it.

Now, I make sure I have a change of scenery that day because the apartment feels really quiet without the noise and energy of a nine-year-old. I'm a freelancer, so I work a lot from home, but I might go into the city and work out of a cafe or catch up with a friend. You have to do something because it is a difficult day.

Ben Dillon-Smith

2 YOUR EX WILL ALWAYS BE IN YOUR LIFE

When there are no kids involved and you have a break up, essentially you just go your separate ways. You need space from that person to purge or get pissed off or do whatever you need to do. But if you've had a kid with someone, you realise, *I'm going to have to spend the rest of my life dealing with this person. And I also have to show my son the right way to behave.* Because there's going to be constant contact.

Every day there's a text coming through: 'You forgot the sports kit.' Or: 'We need to arrange something for this weekend.' It took me a while to get to that point of asking certain questions, like how do we become friends again? How do we maintain some form of relationship? My ex was the one that initiated the break-up and I assumed there was another guy involved because she got together with someone pretty quickly. So all that was playing on my mind. For a while, I was in that passive-aggressive state: *I'm just going to text. I'm just going to email. I don't want to have a conversation with you.*

Letting go was hard. But it's so refreshing when you finally do. It's like a big sigh of relief. Otherwise, it just eats away at you.

For maybe the last six months, I've been in a really good spot with my ex, and I'm happy to talk to her. Recently, she even suggested the three of us go skiing together in Japan. Jethro said, 'It's a little weird.' And I said, 'Yeah, it's a little weird for me too, buddy.'

TFH

3 YOU FIND OUT WHO YOUR REAL FRIENDS ARE

You quickly learn that there are different friends in your friendship group. There are the genuine ones who're actually happy to listen. Then there are the others, who just want to give you advice. All they seem to care about is who've you met on Tinder—it's like they want to live vicariously through your failed dating experiences.

And it'll surprise you which people are truly there for you and which aren't. I have two old friends that I've known since primary school. After the break-up, one of them immediately said, 'If you and Jethro ever need to stay at our place, there's always somewhere here for you.' And the other one? He just kept making suggestions about who he thought I should be sleeping with.

But you need to find people to talk to. It might just be one person; it might be a family member—whoever you feel comfortable with. But you can't do it on your own. You're going to need some help and support.

I actually spoke to a psychologist, too. It was scary and weird—it feels foreign when you're doing that for the first time. It's a big conversation, but it'll help you get through stuff. And sometimes it's better to talk to someone who doesn't know you and won't just go, 'Nah, it's okay. You're alright. She's a bitch.' Sometimes it's better to speak to someone who goes, 'Maybe you need to think about how you handled that.'

Ben Dillon-Smith

4 YOU REALLY APPRECIATE YOUR DAD TIME

When you become a single dad, you possibly think about fatherhood more. Because you're not with your child all the time, it suddenly becomes about making the most of your time together.

I think a lot about creating 'moments' with Jethro. A moment might just be taking a bush walk together or going whale watching. It might be going snorkelling in Vanuatu. Or it could just be sitting on the couch watching David Attenborough. It's just about going, 'Well, I'm with you, let's just create something that's memorable and fun together.'

You appreciate little things, too. When I moved into my new place, my son started wanting to sleep in my bed again for a while. Yes, it can be annoying to be punched in the head through the night by a five-year-old who also does karate, but I'd wake up in the morning with him lying there and think, *This is an amazing moment.*

"Because you're not with your child all the time, it suddenly becomes about making the most of your time together."

TFH

5 DATING AGAIN IS WEIRD

I was with my ex for about twelve years. Dating again after that is strange. When you first download Tinder, you're like, okay, so this is how it works. Now I have to take a photo of myself on a jet ski with my shirt off. And next to a tiger, apparently.

"No matter how bad your situation, no matter how much of a failure you might think you are, your kids still see you as their dad. That is a starting point. It's a chance to turn your life around . . ."

And then you might get to a point where you become a bit too obsessed with Tinder, so you delete it. But then you go back on. Then someone suggests Bumble is better, so you get that, and then you delete both of those apps, and then you come back on them. And then you just end up with Pornhub.

One of the big questions is whether or not you mention you're a single dad in your profile. You see a lot of women on there openly saying; 'I'm a single mum.' Do you do the same?

These days, I actually tend to find myself more aligned with or attracted to other single parents that are on there. There's that level of understanding. Like, 'Yeah, I know, your kid is going to come first and then this is what's available.'

Ben Dillon-Smith

6 TAKE IT EASY ON YOURSELF

You can get into dark spots.
But no matter how bad your
situation, and no matter how much
of a failure you might think you are,
your kids still see you as their dad.
That is a starting point. It's a chance
to turn your life around.

It might take time. And you might
not be able to see your kids as much
as other dads because of your
circumstances. But that can be
fixed and adjusted over time.

When it comes to parenting, you're
not perfect. So just when you think
you know everything, and when you
think you've got it all under control,
you realise that no, you don't. You
learn that a lot as a single dad.

Every week there'll be something
that you forget or something that
you didn't know you had to bring.
His homework or his drumsticks
might be at his mum's place.
Sometimes you'll be able to fix it but
sometimes you won't. That sort of
thing can feed into a sense of failure.

You have to learn not to beat
yourself up. Pat yourself on the back
and say, 'You know what, I got
through today. I did okay. My kid
still loves me; I love them.
There are a shit-load of worse
situations to be in.'

TFH

TEACH YOUR KIDS TO DIG ROCK 'N' ROLL

IN DEFENCE OF THE iPHONE

Many parents are sceptical of you
and your effect, but there is a
moment with you, my iPhone,
that I long for. It is on a plane,
after take-off. I order a drink,
put down my tray-table and plug
you into my laptop.
What happens next is the cascade,
the carousel, the chaos.
Neatly contained within an
aluminium border. It is the unrolling
mosaic of my life. The relentless
rows of small picture tiles advancing
down the screen. Family times.
The microscopic moments that make
up fatherhood. And it is all vibrant
colour; it is smiling teeth, the violent
bloom of bright dresses, the green
of grass, the blue of pools, the tangle
of bodies and limbs. It is everything
I love in this world. It is my family.

"IT'S THE MOST EXCITING TIME IN HISTORY TO BE A DAD."

Professor Richard Fletcher

Father of Caitlin, Chloe and Sophie

Head of the Fathers and Families Research Program at the University of Newcastle / Author of *The Dad Factor*, a book showing how father–baby bonding helps a baby for life.

TFH

For almost twenty years,
I've been travelling to different
communities around Australia
to talk to parents about a father's
role in raising healthy children.
I must have done more than 1500
of those sessions. I've given these
talks for mechanics, police, GPs,
schoolteachers—men from all
sorts of different backgrounds.
And there's one question I always
ask the audience: 'When did you
make the shift from being a boy
to being a man?'

What's the most common answer
from all those men? 'When I became
a father.'

Professor Richard Fletcher

There have been a lot of studies looking at men who've had rough backgrounds—growing up in poverty or abusive families—and exploring how they can escape those social expectations and patterns.

One of the ways the evidence shows they can often get out is by becoming a dad. They might be unlikely to get a really good job, they might be unlikely to go to university, but they can become a dad, and that can give them a whole new sense of self.

It can give them a purpose and a pathway.

But what you do as a father can also affect generations to come. Today, we know from brain mapping that positive fathering (i.e. interacting with your baby with warmth and involvement) affects the chemistry of an infant's brain. It builds up their neural networks and makes those pathways more solid. The networks and pathways that aren't used wither and disappear.

By bonding with their baby, what the father is doing is actually building a network of connections in that infant's brain that will help it socially, help it at school and help it in the world. You can't underestimate what the possibilities are there.

Right now, I think it's the most exciting time in history to be a dad.

I remember thirty-odd years ago when the late former Australian Prime Minister Bob Hawke cried in public after getting a message about his daughter's substance abuse. There were all these newspaper articles saying, 'Has he lost it? Is he falling apart?' Back then, the reaction to showing emotion about your children in public was, 'No way.'

But there's been a really big change. We, as fathers now, have a lot more permission to see ourselves in an emotional way, in an emotional relationship with our children. We're not just expected to pay for things, earn the money and be the disciplinarian. I think we've got more permission now to be emotionally involved.

The drawback, if you like, is that dads have now got to figure it all out. And there are no real blueprints for doing this. New dads, I think, are pioneers. They've got to figure out how to make it all work and find the right balance and they've got to do that without a road map. But they also have more opportunity now than ever before. It's a wonderful time to be a dad.

Professor Richard Fletcher

"By bonding with their baby, the father is actually building a network of connections in that infant's brain that will help it socially, help it at school and help it in the world."

CHILDREN WHO GROW UP WITH INVOLVED FATHERS ARE:

80% less likely to wind up in jail.

75% less likely to have a teen birth.

60% less likely to be expelled
or suspended from school.

Twice as likely to go to university
and find stable employment
after school.

TFH

"PARENTING SEEMS VERY DIFFERENT NOW."

Hugh Jackman

Father of Oscar and Ava

Actor

INTERVIEW BY
Jenny Cooney / HFPA

Before we had kids, Deb and
I made a pretty simple but powerful
choice to look each other in the
eye at every crossroads in life.
Those crossroads are sometimes
big, sometimes they're small,
sometimes you don't even realise
they're crossroads until you look
back. But at those moments,
we said we'd ask each other,
'Is this good or bad for our
marriage?' Or, now that we've got
kids, 'Is this good or bad for our
family?' And as often as possible,
we do the thing that is
good for our family.

Hugh Jackman

Sometimes that can mean doing something for yourself. I don't think it benefits anyone if you're consistently denying yourself something that you love for the sake of the family. No one wants a father or a husband who's miserable.

Parenting seems very different now. I don't ever remember my parents talking to me about what I wanted to study or which university I wanted to go to. I don't even remember my father asking, 'Have you done your homework?' We were left to our own devices to make a lot of decisions. But my father did always talk about the importance of education and I remember a key moment that frustrated me at the time, but looking back now I think was an amazing bit of parenting.

I was offered a job on *Neighbours*, but that same weekend I was also offered a place at the West Australian Academy of Performing Arts, which was a prestigious drama school. So I had this choice: do I go and become a working actor on a two-year contract? Or do I go and study?

I was twenty-four, so I wasn't young in acting terms, and I really didn't know what to do.

I told my father what happened on the Friday and I asked him, 'What should I do?' And he said, 'I can't answer that for you. You have to make your own decision.' I remember going, 'Come on! Make it easy for me. Just tell me what to do!'

By the Sunday, it was really clear to me that I wanted to go and study. I instinctively knew that as an actor, when you're going into an audition, you have to believe in your heart that you deserve to be there. If you don't believe that, you'll never really get the jobs. You might fluke one or two, but you're never going to consistently work if you don't believe that you deserve to be there. And I thought that two years on a soap opera was not going to make me confident enough to go to the Royal Shakespeare Company in London and audition. So I decided to study.

When I told my dad my decision, he said, 'Oh, thank God! I'm so happy you chose that!'

'Why didn't you tell me that?' I said.

'It was your decision,' he said. 'But it's very important that you get educated and go into the world knowing everything you can possibly know. Never stop learning!'

TFH

The difference between
hope and despair
is a good night's sleep.

PRESENT AND CORRECT

"Children don't grow up. They disappear."

– Spike Milligan

Don't wait for the nostalgia to kick in; live in the now.

There is a mistake most parents (including the three of us) make in the way we raise our children: we rush too quickly to the next stage. When your child is barely a suckled creature—waking to feed, then sleeping, then cuddling, then waking to feed again, you might say, 'I wish she could talk to us.'

Then, so soon, they can talk, and we—ready to be free from the bassinet's side—say, 'I can't wait for him to walk!' Of course, mobility, and then an attendant death wish, brings its own set of problems. Day care follows. Kindy. School. Adolescence . . . It all passes in a blur. And with it so does their childhood and their innocence. The child in our kid disappears.

What we might realise, in retrospect, is that we have wished away the cutest, the best, the most precious parts of parenthood—the primal epiphany of providing for a newborn. The sheer fucking wonder the simplest things inspire in a toddler, like a beetle with a colourful stripe on its back, or the miracle of bubbles in fizzy water.

Let's commit to stay in as much of a state of wonder at the world as possible. Let's keep finding the beetles in the grass, even when our kids don't seem to care anymore. If we can keep the child alive in us, still awestruck by the world, there is a good chance our kids will do the same. And isn't that as noble a goal as any?

TFH

GRANDPARENTS ARE THE SUPERHEROES OF MODERN LIFE

Luke Benedictus

Thousands of years of evolution
have fine-tuned an infant's screams
to the exact pitch required to get
a parent's attention. Just to be on
the safe side though, my two-year
-old is cranking up the volume.
Joe howls with a guttural violence
that makes his little body shake.
When I attempt to comfort him,
he furiously shoves me away.
The reason for this rage, for this
nerve-shredding sound?
His ten-month-old brother,
Marc, just cadged a quick go
on his xylophone.

Just as our eardrums begin to throb,
my father-in-law plods into the
bedlam and sizes up the scene.
'Come on, mate,' he says to Joe.
'Want to see some trains?'

TFH

He scoops up Joe with one arm, picks up Marc with the other and plonks them both down on his lap. Seconds later, Joe's tantrum is silenced by a YouTube video of vintage steam trains. The three of them sit happily for the next thirty minutes. Sanity is restored to the house—I'm even able to escape for work.

Here's the thing: little kids love spending time with their grandparents and, thankfully, that feeling tends to be mutual. For some lucky households, this dynamic offers the chance of salvation. Grandparents have become the social glue in modern family life—the support system that stops the whole rickety structure from collapsing. Forget the tired stereotypes of fusty old creatures redolent of pipe smoke and Werther's Originals, grandparents are, in fact, the grey-haired heroes of our time.

They're also more vital than ever. Today's parental landscape, after all, would make Don Draper shudder. Traditional gender stereotypes are dead with stay-at-home mums now an endangered species. The number of families in which both parents work continues to rise; in Australia, the number hovers around 64 per cent. Childcare may be ruinously expensive, but our mortgages are similarly inclined.

That women no longer have to choose between having a career and being a mum is, of course, a just and long overdue correction. But it's not quite as simple as that. Two-income families are inevitably plunged into a maelstrom of extra complications. Whether it's managing sick kids or rush-hour school-runs, the lack of a full-time at-home parent forces you into desperate solutions to stop domestic life morphing into some doleful hybrid of the Fyre Festival and *Lord of the Flies*.

The upshot of all this is greater parental strain. When the Pew Research Center (a US 'fact tank' that monitors the effects of social change) did a study on the functionality of family life, their findings were grimly familiar to every parent who darts about vainly trying to juggle their work and family commitments. In short, what Pew found was that working parents feel stressed, exhausted and rushed off their feet.

Grandparents can help to pick up the slack. They've emerged as the vital cogs in the domestic machine that keep things running, if not always smoothly—there are small kids involved here, remember—then at least formatted into a more tolerable form of anarchy.

Grandparents make it possible for parents to return to work. They alleviate some of the pressure, helping to defer your nervous breakdown and your nightly 'self-medication' tipping into full-blown alcoholism. They step into the breach to rescue you when work presentations collide with ballet-school pick-ups. In short, their support gives your family a chance of maintaining a semi-coherent daily existence.

But their influence goes way beyond practical support. Last night, I returned from work to find Joe stark-naked by the flowerbeds clutching a hosepipe. His grandmother stood at his side, patiently directing his efforts, while he beamed with pride as he doused the hydrangeas. Afterwards, the pair retired to the garden bench to admire their efforts over an ice cream (the relentless distribution of sugary treats has, of course, been every grandmother's modus operandi since the dawn of time, or at least the invention of the Kit Kat).

And that's why grandparents are so invaluable. They're not gun-for-hire babysitters, they are family. As a result, they're truly invested in the welfare of our children. They nurture them with love, affection and quality time while we flap about trying to do far too many things at once (and, often, none of them well).

Given the strength of this bond, it's no wonder that grandparents are proven to be a huge formative influence on our kids. A Cornell University study found that nine out of ten adult grandchildren felt their grandparents had helped to shape their values and behaviours. Sure, on the surface, it looks like they're just force-feeding your kids Tim Tams and letting them win at Connect 4. But in the process, they're inoculating their brains with knowledge, family history, moral scruples and, let's face it, slightly dubious views from a politically correct standpoint.

"Grandparents have become the social glue in modern family life that stops the rickety structure from collapsing."

Luke Benedictus

"Sure, on the surface, it looks like they're just force-feeding your kids Tim Tams and letting them win at Connect 4."

And, thanks to technology, they don't have to live down the road to make their presence felt. My mother may live in England, but she still finds ways to interact. On the brink of her eighties, she's hardly the most tech-savvy, but she still FaceTimes most mornings to check in on her grandsons while they eat breakfast in their highchairs.

On her latest call, it was so cold in my mum's house that she was wearing a woolly hat inside. I held the iPhone steady as she sang 'Twinkle, Twinkle, Little Star'—my two boys watching spellbound, the younger one absent-mindedly smearing a half-chewed mouthful of Weet-Bix into his hair.

Breakfast over, Joe retreated to the sofa but pleaded for Granny to sing 'Baa, Baa, Black Sheep' once more. He was holding the phone, cradling my mother's face in his hands, bewitched by her voice from the other side of the world. Already, she's become a familiar presence in his life. In spite of that great distance, the connection is there.

My sons are lucky enough to still have three living grandparents. But my wife and I are lucky, too.

TFH

MAN vs SANDWICH

When you make a sandwich

With the right bread

(No crust),

Cut into the right shape,

Served on the right

coloured plate,

And still, it goes uneaten;

Know, in this moment,

That your Zen warrior

training has commenced.

Dads spend three times
as many hours a week
with their children as
fathers did in 1965.

Inspiration

"IF YOU SCRATCH THE SURFACE, WE'VE ALL GOT STUFF GOING ON."

Gus Worland

Father of Ella, Abi and Jack

TV / Radio presenter

We need to change the stereotype of what makes a man.

I think a man should be someone who can speak openly about how they feel. If they're going through tough times, they should be able to ask for help and allow people to rally around and support them.

That's really important.

I only realised how important having someone to talk to was after losing my friend Angus to suicide. That led me to make the *Man Up* program on the ABC, which took me around Australia. Until then, I didn't understand how bad men in this country are at talking about things with gravity. We find it really hard to have a conversation outside of the weather, work, sport and maybe a bit of family. And we often make stuff up to make our lives sound better than they actually are.

But why can't men have conversations of gravity where we're talking about our true feelings? At least to one other person who loves us, like our best friend? Why can't we do that?

I think it's because we lack the emotional tools. It goes back for generations: your grandfather never taught your father how to do that, and so he couldn't teach you. So now we're all just blundering around, pretending that we never need help, trying to live up to this stereotype of 'she'll be right, mate'. But it's killing us.

Making *Man Up* changed the way I communicate with my son. When Jack used to ask me a question, if I didn't know the answer I'd try to make it up. I didn't want to seem like someone who didn't know what they were talking about. To me, being a dad meant having all the answers.

But that forced an enormous amount of pressure, not only onto me, but onto Jack, too. One day he asked me something and I said to him, 'I don't actually know, mate. I've been making a lot of this stuff up. I'm just trying my best. I love you. But I don't really know much 100 per cent for sure.'

And Jack said: 'Thank God for that! I thought I had to come up with all the answers all the time.'

'Yeah,' I said. 'Well, that was what I thought, too.'

Gus Worland

So we had this really big moment in our lives where we both just relaxed a lot more in each other's company. We've become more honest and it's been really great for our relationship. For me to become more open is also good for Jack because he realises that everyone's got dramas, everyone is going through things. With most men, if you scratch the surface, we've all got stuff going on. Becoming aware of that makes you realise that we're all just part of one big dysfunctional group of people.

I think suicide is often caused, in part, by loneliness. If you feel lonely you're more likely to maybe make a bad call. But if you're able to realise, *I've got shit going on, but so does my mate. And so does my other mate. We've all got our dramas,* well, that's going to make it easier for you to get through whatever it is you're going through.

The real question though is, how do you find out that your mate is going through a tough time in the first place? You've got to have a proper conversation. But to do that, you've got to spend time with him . . .

It's easy to be isolated from your mates when you become a dad. Suddenly, all your time is focused on looking after your wife, your family, and your work. Before you know it, it's been three months since you've seen your mates. And once you've done three months, it's easy to do six months. Six months becomes a year and all of a sudden, your mates aren't there for you anymore. Or you don't feel that you can do the same things you used to do. You don't go to the footy. You don't have the same conversations as before.

That's why you've got to start making plans to catch up. My wife understands that. Every Sunday morning I go for a walk with my mates, and I make sure my wife does something with her friends, too. And every three months, I go on a boys' trip.

When I come back from those weekends, my wife says I'm a much better husband, father and person because I've just had that time with my mates. Yes, I've been able to carry on a little bit and have some fun. But it also gives me the chance to be there for them.

TFH

"THE BEST PIECE OF ADVICE MY DAD GAVE ME?"

– "YOU CAN'T LIVE IN A CAR."

Tim Cahill

Father of Kyah, Shae, Sienna and Cruz

Former footballer

TFH

My dad, Tim Cahill Senior, was a character. He was from London—a Dagenham boy—and he liked to have a joke. But discipline was a big thing for him, too. He would take me and my two brothers to the park and then make us take off our right boots so we could only kick the ball with our left foot. 'A great footballer has two good feet'—that's what my dad used to say.

As a boy, I used to see the lights flickering in the hallway in the early hours and know my dad was watching the football on TV. I'd sneak out of my bedroom and hide behind the settee to watch too. Dad would let me watch for a while—Serie A or Premier League highlights. And then he'd send me back to bed.

But what I really loved was watching the World Cup on TV with my dad. Watching Schillachi play in Italia '90, that's what got me hooked. And then watching USA '94, and seeing Hagi play for Romania and Bebeto for Brazil! As a kid, it was my dream to play in the World Cup.

Dad worked on fishing trawlers and then went into rigging. But he had a serious injury at work that damaged his hip, and after that he spent a lot of time at home. Dad used to do most of the cooking and was pretty good, too. Chicken schnitzel and pasta with cheese sauce were his specialties.

He made sure my brothers and I became domesticated, too. I'd wash up, one of my brothers would do the drying, we'd do all the vacuuming, make the beds . . . We learned how to work together as a family.

"Becoming a dad was a shock. Before that I was just eat, sleep and focus on football."

Now that I'm a dad, I've become like that with my kids, too. If they want to go to the movies, they have to make sure their room is clean and they've taken out the rubbish. They have to know the value of work.

The best piece of advice my dad gave me was, 'You can't live in a car.' I was signing my first contract at Millwall and I wanted to buy myself a nice new car. But instead, after talking it over, I invested that signing-on fee with my family. My parents and one of my brothers saved up with me, and together we bought our first family home in the outer west of Sydney.

TFH

My parents had taken out a loan to pay for my plane ticket to England for that Millwall trial. And my brother left school to get a job so he could help, too. We've always supported each other because that's what families do.

I was twenty-four when my first son, Kyah, was born. My career was just kicking on and I was about to make my big move to Everton. Becoming a dad was a shock. Before that, I was just eat, sleep and focus on football. Suddenly we had this little man, this little king! I now had serious responsibilities and football started to come second. Becoming a dad changed my whole life and was the best thing that ever happened to me, but it was also my biggest learning curve. Kyah had non-stop colic for the first year, so we didn't get much sleep.

What I find hardest about being a dad is disciplining the kids. You want to be their best mate and you don't want to be the disciplinarian, but you have to sit down with them and have those conversations. I try to relate things back to what it was like for me at their age.

One of my sons wants to be a singer, and one of them wants to a footballer. But my six-year-old told us the other day that he want to be a landscape gardener—I think it's because he likes riding with my dad on his lawnmower.

"When I'm on the sidelines watching my son play football, I say nothing. I don't get involved."

Tim Cahill

When Shae, my thirteen-year-old, told me he wants to be a footballer, I asked him, 'How seriously do you want it?' He said, 'It's all I want to do.' So I said, 'Okay, then let's chase this dream together. But we'll keep some other options open, too.'

What advice would I give another dad when it comes to sport and kids? You have to let them be free. When I'm on the sidelines watching my son play football, I say nothing. I don't get involved. Maybe afterwards I'll give him some advice about positioning or something. But you've got to let them learn for themselves.

One thing I do tell my son though is if he wants to be a footballer, he has to earn it over years and years. It's all about consistency. I tell him: 'If you make sure you're always a seven out of ten in every session, in every game, then you're on the pathway to being a footballer.'

TFH

YOU'RE NOT DOING IT RIGHT.

IF FATHERHOOD HASN'T TURNED YOUR LIFE UPSIDE DOWN,

THE DAILY GRIND

"Any idiot can face a crisis; it's this day-to-day living that wears you out."

– Anton Chekhov*

Feed, change, bathe, rock, clean, repeat . . . Endurance is part of the parental deal.

Parenting is often another word for next-level drudgery. You know that already, of course. But just in case you're in denial—and you have to be to some extent—here are some corroborating facts from a survey of 2000 British parents. (And yes, these stats seem to err on the conservative side.)

Before your child is four years old, you'll change their nappy a staggering 3738 times.

You'll have to tame 1092 tantrums, and your child will push away their uneaten food 288 times.

That old 'it's a marathon, not a sprint' adage doesn't really cut it where parenting is concerned. It's more like an extreme triathlon performed on your knees. Fatherhood requires you to reconcile yourself with a particular kind of monotony. Whether you're pacing the yard at 3:30 a.m. trying to rock your baby to sleep, or reading *Spot's Day Out* for the twenty-third night straight, there is a relentlessness to being a dad.

How to put a positive spin on this? Well, for starters, it may be good for your soul. Repetition is central to almost every form of devotional life, from Benedictine prayer to Buddhist mantras. A spiritual practice is built upon endless routine until some flicker of the divine shimmers through the mundane. Repetition encourages the dissolution of the ego and a form of selflessness to take hold.

Too mystical? Okay, try this then: sometimes, the most tiresome acts of parenting are brightened by something truly special. From your child's first steps to a delicious fit of the giggles, such moments aren't predictable—you'll only catch them if you're there.

All those nappy-changing, tantrum-taming stints will only deepen your relationship with your kids, and, suffice to say, that's worthwhile. You don't want to end up a stick figure in your child's life (except in their kindergarten drawings).

*This quote is always attributed to Chekhov, but no source has ever been found. Quote boffins still debate whether the Russian writer, Clifford Odets, or Bing Crosby uttered the original line. We reckon the source was a frazzled parent who lost concentration after yet another broken night's sleep.

TFH

Better Fathers ⟵

→ **Better Families**

Q. WHAT'S THE MOST IMPORTANT THING A NEW DAD CAN DO?

A. TAKE PARENTAL LEAVE.

Pete Rhodes

Father of Harvey and Liam

Director at PWC

When Harvey was born, I never really got the chance to spend any significant time with him to make that initial connection. He was born in December, so I was able to take some time over Christmas—I probably had four weeks off work. That left Clare, my wife, dealing with parenthood almost on her own to a degree. It was quite a tumultuous time.

When Liam was about to come along, I had a couple of chats with people at work and it transpired that they were incredibly supportive of dads taking time off. So I leapt at the opportunity. They offered 18 weeks of parental leave at full pay, and I took that leave when Liam was born.

It was such a great opportunity to experience that hands-on parenting in the first formative months of Liam's life. Taking parental leave has certainly given me a stronger bond with my kids. But it made me more confident, not only as a parent, but also as a person.

I used to think that my work was stressful, but having to manage two boys under three years old gives you a fresh perspective. I came back to work feeling totally blissful and Zen. Now, there's hardly anything in a work context that gets me too stressed. It's far harder to bring children up than to manage very important people at work.

"Taking parental leave built trust and solidified our relationship as a true partnership."

Taking parental leave was also extremely positive for my relationship. It meant I was able to experience firsthand a lot of the things that Clare had been going through with Harvey the first time around. Looking after a baby is quite monotonous and difficult. It's pretty easy to keep a little baby alive, but it's much harder to keep them constantly stimulated, happy and satisfied, and do all that in a way that means you don't also lose your mind.

Taking parental leave has made it a bit easier to deal with those moments where you're both tearing your hair out. And I think it means that there's less chance of those moments snowballing into problems within the relationship. Being at home with the baby meant that I was able to empathise more with my wife and properly understand her frustrations. This meant I was able to support her more. I could anticipate moments much quicker and know what I really needed to do around the house in order to be more helpful. Because the first time around, you haven't got a clue and you generally get it all wrong.

Taking parental leave built trust and solidified our relationship as a true partnership. We bring our children up as partners. We're both genuinely sharing the parenting roles: we both work full-time and we both bring our kids up with a lot of help from a very expensive day-care system. (I do think the cost of childcare in Australia is prohibitive and the government's got a lot of work to do to address that issue.)

I'm pretty confident that if I hadn't taken the leave, Clare would've found it harder to get back into work. But after about four weeks, she was able to work from home part-time. That was really good for her, as she wasn't having to commute and didn't have to leave Liam—because obviously he still needed to feed. But one or two days a week, she could shut herself away in the home office and get back into her work. I'd look after both the boys and we'd have a total riot.

I'm now a lot more aware of some of the broader community issues that we need to try and change. There's still a huge stigma attached to dads taking extended leave. There's a bit of that old-school approach of it's the woman's job and the woman's role. That absolutely needs to be quashed.

Pete Rhodes

But there are also worrying statistics about how difficult it is for a woman to get back into the workforce if she doesn't have partner who's also able to take some time off. In places like Sweden, where it's the norm for dads to take parental leave, it's not a problem for women to get back into the workforce. And the quicker they can do that, the quicker they can get back on the corporate ladder and the fewer opportunities they lose.

What advice would I give someone who worked for a company with a less-enlightened parental leave policy? It's really difficult. I was lucky. I can sit here and bullshit you and say I'd tell him to demand that his employer grants him parental leave, but things don't work like that in the real world. What I would say is that corporates are not going to change their minds unless enough people do the same thing.
We need to demonstrate that the change is required.

You could start by getting some guidance from a network of people that have been through the process. Get some ideas as to how you can go and talk to your employer and try and change their mind. In an extreme scenario, you could try and find a competitor that offers it, confront your employer and say 'Look, I want this leave.

"It made me more confident not only as a parent, but also as a person."

'If you're not going to give me parental leave then I've got an offer for a job over here. What would you rather I do?' Statistically, companies with better parental leave packages get better staff retention. Their staff are likely to be more loyal, more content, and also far better at getting their job done in a very short space of time, hence they will be more efficient. So, it should save employers money in the long run by accepting the very short-term cost.

As far as my experience went, there was no downside to taking parental leave whatsoever—there were only positives. Bringing up children can be stressful at times. There's no manual, so you've basically got to make it up as you go along. But when you're both sharing that, you are genuinely sharing parenthood rather than just allowing one of the parents to assume that role. It sets the framework for the way you want to do things going forward. You want to be parents together throughout your child's life. So why not start out that way?

TFH

HOW A CARTOON DOG BECAME THE ULTIMATE GUIDE TO FATHERHOOD

Luke Benedictus

Modern fatherhood has
a new icon. Forget George
Clooney (too slick), Jamie
Oliver (too busy) or The Rock
(looks too much like a thumb).
No, the father figure any
man should now model their
dad-game on is, in fact,
a cartoon dog from the
Brisbane suburbs.

Bandit is the dad in *Bluey*, the hugely successful animation series that's leapfrogged *Play School* and *The Wiggles* to become the number one show in ABC iView history. It charts the domestic life of the titular character, a blue-heeler pup who lives with her parents and four-year-old sister, Bingo, in Brisbane.

For a kids' TV show, this setting is significant. *Bluey* unfolds in a world of lorikeets, backyard barbies and jacaranda trees. In short, it's a homegrown series that's as fair-dinkum as the late former Australian Prime Minister Bob Hawke skulling a beer at the Boxing Day Test.

'I wanted to get an Australian feel that wasn't the outback and kangaroos and koalas,' explains Joe Brumm, the series creator. 'I just thought that's pretty well-worn. What I wanted was suburban Australia.'

Equally refreshing is *Bluey*'s take on fatherhood. Bandit is a laid-back but resourceful dad who's heavily involved in the day-to-day childcare. In his home office, he sits on a yoga ball at his desk because, as he explains to Bluey, 'I wrecked my back changing your nappies.' From cleaning to washing to school runs, Bandit navigates the drudgery of household life with calm assurance. 'He's actually really competent,' Brumm says. 'He's a good dad.'

In the animated universe, this makes him something of a rarity. After all, from King Thistle to Homer Simpson, cartoon dads tend to be halfwits or buffoons. The father in *Peppa Pig* is a textbook example. Daddy Pig is a good-natured glutton with a 'big tummy', whose efforts at map-reading, barbecuing and DIY (the stereotypical mainstays of paternal expertise) always end in disaster. Asked to draw a picture of a vegetable to take in to school, Peppa sketches her dad slumped in front of the TV.

TFH

Not everyone laughs off all this 'silly daddy' stuff either. In a survey by mothering website *Netmums*, 93 per cent of parents agreed that the media depiction of dads failed to reflect what they contribute to real family life. Almost half said that such portrayals could make kids think that dads are 'useless' while 28 per cent claimed the shows were a 'very subtle form of discrimination' and that there'd be uproar if the same jokes levelled at dads were fired at women, ethnic minorities or religious groups.

Eyed from this context, Bandit's character seems loaded with extra significance. Is he a four-legged counter-attack for gender equality? The truth is actually far more heartening: Bandit, it turns out, isn't some figure of political allegory, but a straight-up depiction of the here and now.

The inspiration for *Bluey* is primarily observational, Brumm explains. In that respect, Bandit's approach to parenting simply reflects the animator's own experience and that of his circle of brothers and mates.

'He's like every sort of caring dad these days,' Brumm says. 'They're across everything—the housework, kids, work, the lot. Compared to my dad's day, we've just had a slow, generation-by-generation change to the point we're at now, where being a dad just seems like an all-in.'

Bluey is heavily biographical, with Brumm sharing many characteristics with Bandit. He's the father of two small girls, too, and, in the running of his own animation company, he largely worked from home in their early years to become an active figure in their daily lives. 'I mean, Bandit is a much better dad than me,' he says. 'But when I write a cartoon, I can obviously cut out the shortcomings that I have as a dad, which are definitely numerous.'

"We've just had a slow, generation-by-generation change to the point we're at now, where being a dad just seems like an all-in."

Bluey **was still in embryonic form when Brumm's eldest daughter started school. Her experience changed the course of the show . . .**

Yet there's one area, Brumm concedes, where *Bluey* does get 'vaguely political'. The cartoon resolutely champions the importance of play.

'Play time was suddenly taken away from her, it was just yanked and seeing the difference in her was horrendous,' he says. 'There was no playing, there was no drawing, it was just straight into all this academic stuff. And the light in her eyes just died.'

The family subsequently changed their daughter's schooling after Brumm began to research the value of play for child development. Mastering these soft kindergarten skills, he found, is a vital stage in kids' evolution into socially aware creatures. Their make-believe games can deliver self-taught but powerful lessons about how to cooperate, share and interact.

'*Bluey* is just one long extrapolation of that,' Brumm says. 'It's to encourage people to look at play not just as kids mucking around, but as a really critical stage in their development that, I think, we overlook at their peril.'

This shift in focus had a massive impact on the show. Zeroing in on imaginative play and the wacky scenarios this threw up helped to unlock *Bluey*'s creative potential while maintaining its observational stance. Crucially, it also allowed Bandit to maintain a degree of dignity while still being a comical character.

The father plays a central role in these madcap games with his kids. One minute he's pretending to be a magic claw vending machine; the next he's immersed in an Indiana Jones-style adventure dodging a giant yoga ball.

TFH

'But because the show is so focused on play, it's perfectly fine that someone who is a confident and caring dad could just switch into these Monty Python scenarios and not be a complete fall-guy and moron,' Brumm explains. 'You believe it and the kids still laugh at it. But you're left with a more nuanced character, one who you can respect for his dedication and who you can also laugh at.' Yet while *Bluey* is a show about play, that doesn't mean it's all fun and games for the adults. This isn't a saccharine portrayal of fatherhood; Bandit's coat is flecked with grey hairs for a reason. The show refuses to flinch from the fact that parenting is bloody hard work.

Bandit never gets to do anything he wants to as his desires are constantly surrendered to the whims of family life. Attempts to read the newspaper or work from home are invariably sabotaged by the kids. When Bandit and his brother try to watch the cricket, they're forced to play 'horsey weddings' instead. The selflessness that fatherhood demands is made explicit in the episode 'Fruitbat'. Bluey creeps downstairs one night to find her dad fast asleep with a rugby ball tucked under his arm.

Bandit, we see, is literally dreaming of playing sport and hanging out with his mates. 'He doesn't get to play touch-football anymore because he's busy working and looking after you,' his wife explains.

'When you become a dad, you are propelled into one of the biggest periods of learning and sacrifice in your life,' says Brumm. 'Suddenly, the last vestiges of your selfishness are just thrown to the wind. When the kids come along it's like, 'Well, your wants and needs are now completely irrelevant. You're here to provide.

'For me, that was quite difficult. And we try and show that with Bandit. In an episode like 'Fruitbat', the point was to show all the things he really wants to do that he doesn't get to do. There are a few echoes of longing from him, but there's not a trace of regret. Bandit is happy with the trade he's made. He's accepted it. And it's such a beautiful trade.'

Brumm knows what he's talking about from his own experience of fatherhood. Between emergency trips to intensive care, asthma attacks and 'real bad sleep', family life has often proved a bumpy ride.

'Since becoming a dad, it seems like I've faced more major problems in the last eight years than I had in the previous thirty-two,' he laughs. 'Sometimes I just think, 'My god, it's like I've started some post-graduate degree in pain.'

'But I love who I've become because of it. I mean, obviously, I've got these kids, which is great. But I've also become so much tougher. I could never have done something of the scale of *Bluey* without being through those experiences and that process of hardening up.'

Such reflections on parenthood quietly inform the show. Scattered through the episodes gleam bright moments of paternal inspiration. They're apparent in an episode like 'Takeaway', when a straightforward trip to the local Chinese turns into a slapstick disaster. Kids need the toilet at tricky moments; a tap faucet gets stuck, the long-awaited food ends up scattered in the gutter.

But just as Bandit begins to despair, a fortune cookie delivers some timely perspective on the fleeting nature of childhood. 'Sometimes you need those reminders,' says Brumm. He mentions the episode 'Bike' in which Bluey is struggling to learn how to ride her bike while her friends encounter their own playground complications. (Spoiler alert: perseverance ultimately pays off.) Yet Brumm says of that episode, 'If there is any type of message, it's aimed at the adults rather than the kids.'

'That episode was really just about my experience of parenting,' he says. 'It's really hard, it's quite brutal, but you just keep turning up. You just keep trying, and hopefully, it all works out. Don't give up.'

It's a message that delivers more reassurance than any childcare manual. When you're waist-deep in the swirling chaos, fatherhood can feel like a battle to keep your head above water. But as Bandit—the spirit animal of the modern dad shows—you can always resort to doggy-paddle.

"When you become a dad, you are propelled into one of the biggest periods of learning and sacrifice in your life."

1970

6

Total number of American
men who defined themselves
as stay-at-home dads.

2014

→ **2,000,000**

Fatherhood changes everything. It changes the texture of your marriage and your conception of time. It changes your approach to work and play. Fatherhood changes how you feel about the

spatial dimensions of your car. It changes your brain chemistry, your sense of urgency, the trajectory of your dreams. Fatherhood changes you for the better.

FAMILY VALUES

"For unflagging interest and enjoyment, a household of children, if things go reasonably well, certainly makes all other forms of success and achievement lose their importance by comparison."

— Theodore Roosevelt

Just become a dad?
Prepare for your life priorities
to be scrambled. Forever.

Admittedly, there's a polite
disclaimer in Roosevelt's quote
('if things go reasonably well').
But the twenty-sixth president
of the United States was on
to something here. Forget the
tantrums. Forget the felt-tip mural
scribbled on the wall. Forget the
trip to hospital after that baked
bean refused to budge from that
child-sized nostril.

When your kids are happy and
behaving with vague decorum,
family life can sometimes induce
a truly heart-warming effect on
your soul.

It can make a mockery out of
your former priorities, too. That
promotion at work? That second
house? That nagging desire to climb
a mountain, fly a Cessna or live
overseas? After fatherhood, such
bucket-list dreams move into the
'bonus' category. Children bring
with them a sledgehammer of
perspective with which to flatten
life into a more lucid form, albeit
one covered in grubby fingerprints
and My Little Pony stickers.

TFH

LIVE SO THEY LOOK UP TO YOU, HOWEVER BIG THEY GROW

SO, WHERE'S THE MUM?

Harold David

Father of twins Henry and Frankie

Artist / Photographer

I always knew that
I wanted to be a dad.
It's weird. I never even
thought it wasn't a
possibility. But in my
situation, as a gay man,
it's not something that
just happens by chance,
you know? It's not like
a random act that takes
place in the back of
a Chevy. It has to be really
planned and thought out.

I was with my ex for fifteen years, but he never wanted to be a dad. He always said, 'If you have a kid, I'll be the uncle.' And I'd think, *Okay, I don't know how that's going to work.*

But in 2007, while we were still together, I went to LA and started the surrogacy process there. I gave this doctor a deposit of money and 'baby-making ingredients', and then the ass fell out of the economy and the Australian dollar took a nosedive. What was going to cost me around $100,000 was suddenly going to cost me $200,000, and the insurance costs went up, too. I just couldn't do it. But then India started opening their doors to overseas surrogacy.

In 2011, by pure synchronicity, I was watching Jenny Brockie's *Insight* show, and they were interviewing this woman called Dr Shivani, who ran the most reputable surrogacy agency in India. I loved her philosophy and everything about what she said. I contacted her the next day and was over there in two weeks and starting the process.

The difference this time was that I was single (I broke up with my ex in 2009). For the next year and a half, I worried about whether I could make it work as a single dad. But I kept thinking about it and everything kept leading me in the same direction. Finally I decided that I wasn't going to let being single stop me from becoming a dad.

Not only was I single, I was also working a lot—this was at the height of my fashion photography work. My friends said to me, 'Are you crazy?' But I'd remind them of that saying: 'If you want to get a job done, give it to a busy person.' So, I was in that mode and I still am. Plus, the truth was that I was forty-nine, so it felt like now or never.

And then I had my twin boys . . .

"Every night after the boys go to bed, I always look in on them while they're sleeping, and my heart just . . . I almost get a little tear in my eye."

Harold David

My mum came over from Austin, Texas for two months and she helped out at first. Then I was on my own. I can barely remember that first year now. It's almost like when a woman has a baby and she forgets the pain of labour and two years later wants to have another child. I forget what those early months were like, the sheer craziness of it all. But at least with twins it's like it all happens in one big swoop. You just double everything and it's all the same: the same feeding times, the same nap times, it's just increasing the load. Where I was lucky was that both Henry and Frankie were great sleepers.

I had a nanny on-call who lived nearby. She would come and help out if any big jobs came through. Then she went to college and couldn't do it anymore, so I built a granny flat in the back (we called it the 'nanny flat') and we had a live-in nanny.

I had really thought that was it for relationships. I was resigned to being single. But eight months after they were born, I brought the kids into a bistro for lunch and Andy was our waiter. We've been together ever since. Andy is a second dad to them. He's been instrumental in raising these kids.

How has fatherhood changed me? I've learned how to be patient; I've learned how to listen. In a way, I'm sterner now. Before, I'd always been kind of lax with anything that's regimented, like being on time. But in the last couple of years, I've realised that I need to teach the boys some boundaries.

I'm also a lot softer in many ways now. Every night after the boys go to bed, I always look in on them. Even if it's been a long day, I look in on them while they're sleeping, and my heart just . . . I almost get a little tear in my eye. Yeah, I'm definitely softer.

TFH

Has becoming a father made me a better man? I guess so, because I think a better man is someone who doesn't necessarily just take on the traditional roles of fatherhood. When I was a kid, my dad never changed my nappy, never cooked a meal, he never did any of that. The newer generations of dads—we're so much more in-tune with the needs of a child. Our involvement isn't so restricted.

Looking back, my dad was pretty absent most of the time. We lived in Detroit until I was fourteen and Dad was a pipe fitter at the Ford Motor Company. He worked in the factory. But there were two things he always did with me: one was play guitar and sing, and the other was toss a baseball.

Last Christmas, I got each of my boys a baseball glove and a baseball. That's one of the things that I most love doing with them: teaching them how to catch and throw.

What would I advise a guy going into surrogacy? Make sure you're ready. Make sure you've gotten a lot of things out of your system.

But the most important thing for me is that I still paint. I've got my first exhibition this year, and I still do photography. Doing that is a struggle for me because I do have some guilt around it. But then I listened to this kind of guru, her name's Marianne Williamson, and she said something that stuck with me. She said, 'It's really important for your kids to see you doing what you love to do that's not necessarily related to them.' Hearing her say that helped to get me over the guilt. So that's what I'd say to anyone going into surrogacy or becoming a dad in general: just keep being yourself.

What's really funny about being a gay dad is that 99.9 per cent of the people you meet are just so on board with it. I have not had one person say anything negative to me. Not one.

Harold David

"I had really thought that was it for relationships. I was resigned to being single. But eight months after they were born, I brought the kids into a bistro for lunch and Andy was our waiter. We've been together ever since."

Four years ago, I was in Marfa, Texas with Andy and the boys. We were pushing the twins in a double pram and suddenly this older guy—he must've been seventy—pulled up and stopped in front of us in his pick-up truck with all these rifles stacked in the back window. The man got out of his truck, stood right in front of us and looked us up and down, then said, 'So, where's the mum?'

I looked at Andy, 'cause Andy's a pretty big guy, and I thought, *Okay, well, here we go!*

But Andy just said, 'No, we're two dads.'

This guy's whole face just completely softened. He looked at us and then he nodded. 'Well,' he said. 'It looks like you're doing a good job.'

And then he got back into his pick-up truck and drove off.

83% of millennial dads say that family is more important than their career.

"I AM DEFINITELY GOING TO DO WHATEVER IT TAKES FOR MY FAMILY."

John Krasinski

Father of Hazel and Violet

Actor / Writer / Director

INTERVIEW BY
Jenny Cooney / HFPA

I had the greatest father in the world, so I just wanted to be him. I mean, my goal in life (and I truly mean this—all this Hollywood business aside) is to be a quarter as good of a person as he is. If I can do that, then I win. So I have always looked up to him and tried to be like him.

I remember when I was young and someone explained chivalry to me. I was like, 'What is chivalry?' And this guy said, 'It's like holding doors open and letting a woman into a car before you.' And that whole idea was just so obvious to me because my dad always did those things.

"I had the greatest father in the world."

I think the idea of protecting and providing for your family is definitely inside me because of him. I am a protector and a provider, going back to the sort of hunter/gatherer idea; I know I am definitely going to do whatever it takes for my family.

TFH

THE BEST THING
TO SPEND ON
YOUR KIDS
IS YOUR TIME

"FATHERHOOD CAN BE YOUR OPPORTUNITY TO REDEFINE WHO YOU ARE."

Thomas Docking

Father of Evelyn, Annabelle and Joseph

CEO of Dads Group Inc, an organisation that connects
new dads and families in local communities — dadsgroup.org

The way I used to think of shock
was like that zap you got if you licked
a nine-volt battery. Then I found out
my wife was pregnant. That redefined
what shock was for me.

It was completely unplanned.
My wife, Kate, and I had just sold
everything we owned to go on a trip
around the world—we were going
to be away for two to three years.
We started on Hayman Island and
from there we were planning to go
to the Caribbean, to South America,
and on to all these other places.
But this news meant we had to
make a massive U-turn.

Kate said I didn't really talk for two weeks. What was going through my mind? Imagine putting your head into a giant church bell and then someone hitting it.
What goes through your mind is a whole lot of sound, a whole lot of noise and a whole lot of nothing. You're bewildered—that's what shock is. There's this sense of disconnection. It's like all the plugs have suddenly been pulled out of the back of your cranium.

Because we'd either sold or given away everything to move overseas on this trip, we came back home to nothing. It could have been a really difficult and lonely experience for us as a couple, but thanks to the generosity of our family and community, we were okay. Someone helped us out with a house with subsidised rent, we were given furniture, and stuff for the baby. So I didn't really need to buy anything. And it got me thinking: 'Man, imagine if I was nineteen and having a kid and I didn't have any family.'

But that happens every day. There are 300,000 babies born a year in Australia. Many of those are to new dads who don't have any sort of support whatsoever. Realising that made me ask, how can there be no support for all these dads?

Failing to support these guys means we're not equipping them to support the mums. That's how Kate and I went down the path of setting up an organisation to support new fathers in a really practical way.

Lots of dads are initially kind of lost. Life with a new baby can make you feel like you're failing on multiple fronts as a man. Often, your capacity to work is limited because you're so tired. You can feel like you're failing at home because you're comparing yourself to your wife, who's probably spent more hours a day with your child, so she's increasing her capability and confidence way faster than you are. Then you're failing with your local community because you don't have time for your friends anymore, so you're not out in the pub or surfing or playing footy.

Thomas Docking

What's happening is that your previously defined metrics for success have been ripped out from underneath you. If you don't change those metrics, you're probably going to keep feeling like a failure in all these areas of your life.

You need to do two things: firstly, spend time with other new dads (with your infants) to give your partner a break and to help establish a new baseline. Secondly, redefine what success looks like for you in the context of fatherhood.

The greatest thing about redefining success is that it becomes personal to you and your family's own situation and values. It doesn't matter if you're a CEO, if you're unemployed, or if you're a tradie or a surgeon. Your fatherhood experience has to be defined by you and your partner.

"Every father has his own game to play, and every single one of them can win."

And this is a very special thing. If you realise and recognise this, it can be a real opportunity. Fatherhood can be your opportunity to redefine who you are and where you want to succeed. Every father has his own game to play, and every single one of them can win.

Everyone's metrics are different. I've got a friend in my dads' group who lives in Melbourne (Victoria) and does fly-in, fly-out work in Karratha (Western Australia). Being home for bath time every night isn't going to work as a metric for him. But when he's back at home for two weeks, his metric of success might be, say, teaching his child to paint or to grow a veggie garden. And his metrics aren't possible for me to emulate on a Wednesday afternoon because I'm in meetings. So your metrics should be tangible, but they also need to be personalised to your family.

You also need to be setting goals that you can achieve easily. Because you've got less sleep, you've got less focus, you've got fewer resources and you've got less energy. Consequently, you need to set simple goals. Set your expectations super-high and you're really going to struggle through the next ten years of trying to be a great dad, trying to earn more money, trying to do this and that. You'll set yourself up to fail.

TFH

Whereas if you consider your value in this family space, it's easier to succeed on those metrics. You can make sure you're checking the box on being a great father, checking the box on being a great partner. Whatever 'great' means to your family unit, whether it's being a stay-at-home dad or earning the money to put food on the table.

Too often we end up comparing our situation to other people. We pull up at the lights in our car, look left and check out the car next to us. The next moment we're starting to judge our own car and judge our own life in comparison, and then that car drives away. But you can't take that approach. You have to just go, 'Hey, this is our vehicle, this is our life, this is our family, this is where we're going.'

You just have to accept that you're doing your best in whatever circumstances you're in right now as a dad. That's what you're asked to do, because that's what you can do. Maybe you can't spend lots of time with your kid because you're travelling overseas or you're living away from them. But you can still write a letter. There's always something you can do.

Now is such a great time to be a dad. If you look at previous generations of fathers, many of them never even changed nappies. So there was a connection that wasn't there between father and infant in that culture. But things have changed

We have so much information now, and we have such an opportunity to pioneer new ways of raising a family. Many men want to do something that's unique and different, and they're chasing that out in the world. But when you become a dad, the opportunity is right there to come back and redefine with your partner what you're going to do as a father—how you're going to accept that responsibility and how you're going to enjoy the most precious thing in the world.

"Life with a new baby can make you feel like you're failing on multiple fronts."

Thomas Docking

Your children can offer the most amazing reset for your life. Sometimes you need to restart your phone, sometimes you need to restart your computer, and sometimes you need to restart your day. Your kids can help you do that. You can have all this baggage on your to-do list or all these angry managers screaming at you down the phone, and then you pick up your child and it's like, 'Whew! That's right. It's not about all that other stuff. It's about this life and it's about appreciating that.'

After picking up my child, I can go back into that storm with a smile on my face. I can smile with the rain smashing into me and just go, 'Alright, I'll get through this one because it's not the main game. The main game is back there at home. This is just a whole bunch of noise and stress. I'll get through it just like I got through all the other noise and stress in the last thirty years.'

Picking up your child can help you remember that everything that life's got for you exists in that little family unit. It can help to remind you that you don't want to spend your life running too fast in the wrong direction.

"You don't want to spend your life running too fast in the wrong direction."

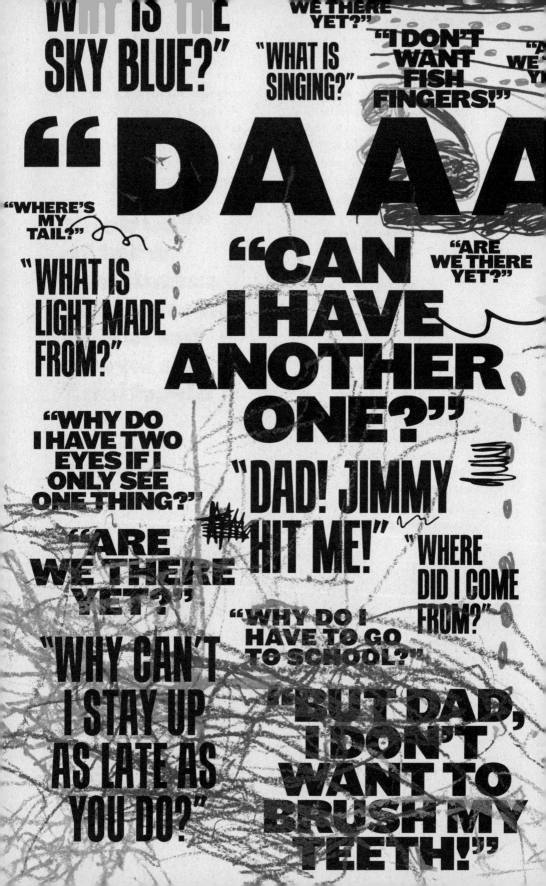

• AM
PM

• ALARM

WHEN THE HOUSE IS QUIET

A father's relationship with silence
Is deep
And precious.

What was once, in years before,
An absence of sound
Is now a presence, with luxurious qualities.
Rare enough to be truly appreciated when it comes.

In the same way that silence between friends
Can be more companionable than conversation,

Silence for a father can be like clouds clearing from
Around the moon.

It can illuminate the lay of the land, and quickly connect him
To valuable places.

In silence, a father can find space (in a crowd).
In silence, a father can find stillness (amidst chaos).

In silence, a father can find himself
As he is now,
As he was before,
And as he wants to be tomorrow.

TFH

"WHEN THERE'S A BREAKDOWN IN A RELATIONSHIP AND THEN THERE'S A BLENDED FAMILY, YEAH, IT'S CHALLENGING."

Commando Steve Willis

Father of Brianna, Ella, Jack and Axel

Personal trainer / TV personality

TFH

My stepdad ('Dad' to me) grew

up in the tail end of the era when

children were seen but not heard.

He met my mum when I was five.

And with me not being his own

child, and then three other sons

coming along, well, I think there

was a lot going on for him within

his own head.

Commando Steve Willis

When that happens, there's not much room, space or time for anything else. As a child coming into that situation, you can quite easily magnify your parent's agitation or be a tipping point for it.

So there wasn't a whole lot of leniency where my dad was concerned. It was very much 'My way or the highway'. He was very, very strict.

But you start to understand your dad better as you get older. There's a recognition that he was just doing the best that he could. And, like many of us, we're victims of our own suffering.

I believe there was a lot of uncertainty for him, and he very much lived his life with his body armour on, so that expression of emotion and that more gentle way of being wasn't shown too often.

As a child, I saw that example as a constant, so then I thought, *Well that's how I need to be as an adult.* My dad was so quick to anger, and he used anger as a means of quelling a situation. But later I realised that there was another way.

Brianna was born when I was twenty-two, so I was still young and very much like a dog chasing its tail. Your ego gets the better of you. I remember, as a young dad with Brianna, certain circumstances where I would almost be like this big scary monster to show her who was the boss.

But then Ella and Jack came along in my thirties, and there was a point when I had a conversation with myself about how I wanted to be there for my kids as a dad. I suppose that I wanted to do things differently to how I felt my parents had approached raising me. I didn't want to perpetuate a lot of fear and, to a degree, the ignorance that's born out of fear.

If you can be gentle, if you can be kind, if you can harness those emotions—then why not be that way as a dad? Why would you want to be anything other than that?

Dad was a small-engine mechanic
and what I learned from him was
to work hard. But what I've done
with that message is work hard,
not just in the sense of getting up
and clocking in, but in all aspects
of life. I'm trying to be a role model,
a mentor, and a better parent.
I try to show my children that,
as a male, as a man, as a father,
that nothing is below me. So I'll get
in there and clean the toilets, wash
the dishes, cook the food and make
the beds. But I'll also do those
things with pride, because I think
children are ever-present and
always watching.

Dad was big on respect. He just
wanted his boys to grow up being
willing to go above and beyond for
anybody, really. That emphasis on
making a contribution was
something that he did, not so
much in words, but very much in
his actions.

Being in the military as a dad,
I didn't know anything different,
and I didn't really question any other
way of being. And then I started to
listen to mates who were a little
older—into their late twenties and
thirties. They had kids and were still
in the army, and this started to raise
a lot of questions for them, with all
the time away. I left the military in
2004, and there have been a lot of
deployments since then . . . Guys
would have had to do those and be
away for a minimum of six months
at a time, and that would be hard.

As a parent, creating some space
for yourself can really help you cope.
If you can just take some time out,
even if it's five or ten minutes,
to take a few deep breaths, then it
can really calm things down.
I think so many of the things we do
in the heat of the moment happen
because we're tired and we're short
of that mental space. It just takes
a bit of defiance from a child and
before you know it, you're on them.
Then there's the guilt and the
questioning: *Why did I do that?*

TFH

I've been using meditation for years. Like before I came here, I'd been driving around everywhere then I took Axel to day care, and he just dead-set didn't want to go. He was in tears. I nearly brought him home because I was just feeling so much for him. And I could feel all this tension within myself, so I took about 12 minutes, and just sat down and crossed my legs in a quiet area and breathed in and out. I focused on my in-breath and just connected with myself. Breathing in, I'm aware that there's tension in my body. Breathing out, I calm and ease the tension.

When there's a breakdown in a relationship and then there's a blended family, yeah, it's challenging. It requires teamwork, and teamwork needs cohesion, connection and for bonds to form. This can take years. What I've learned from my own personal experience is that it requires compromise. We need to provide each other more breathing space in times of need rather than just projecting our thoughts and opinions into a situation. Providing that space can enable us to find calm, practical solutions that benefit everyone.

I think there's been a big shift in the status quo around just putting up with a relationship for the children's sake. If you can't work things out, it's more socially acceptable nowadays to go your separate ways, but to still be unified as parents. We understand that.

But once you move beyond that understanding you've got to figure out how that actually works in the practical sense. I think we're all fumbling in the dark a lot more than we'd probably like to admit.

There's no easy solution. You want to spend time with your kids. You want to make that relationship with your partner work. You want to make the relationship work with children that potentially aren't yours. But then you've got the additional responsibilities of work and bringing money in to support your family. It becomes really difficult.

I think a lot of people find it hard
to accept their circumstances.
But with acceptance, we can let
certain things go. That creates the
space for us to be able to deal with
what needs to be dealt with.

The other day I heard about this
lady. Her twin sister ended up sick
and in a coma, and when she woke
up, she had a brain injury. Ever since
that day, her father gave up
everything else to be a full-time
carer for his daughter. If there's
a superhero in this world, it's
someone like that. That takes
strength. That takes bravery.
To grind it out each day, over and
over again, and be there for your kin.
Man, that's noble.

There's this Zen Buddhist master,
Thich Nhat Hanh, who's written a
book called *No Mud, No Lotus*.
Without the mud, the lotus
wouldn't exist. The lotus is
beautiful; it's a flower and it sits on
top of the water, but where is it
anchored? It's anchored in the mud.
It's through our suffering, and
transforming our suffering, that
we see the beauty. That relates
to parenting.

I'm in my forties now, but I've
observed people who are older than
me and seen their conflict with
coming to terms with the later
stages of life and being faced with
death. That's made me recognise
that I want to have as much quality
time and as many experiences
with my kids as possible because,
before I know it, I'll be at that
doorstep, too.

The older I get, the more I realise life
is all about the human interaction.

RED ALERT

"Govern a family as you would cook a small fish: very gently."

– Chinese proverb

In our hyper-accelerated age, patience is more of a virtue than ever.

There are a lot of hot moments in the process of running a family. Burning, crazy, seeing-red moments, like when—on all fours—you again manage to kneel on that one floorboard near the door that goes 'creeeeaaak' and wake the baby.

Or when, for the eighth time that night, your toddler decides to get up and stand unsteadily on the kitchen table to sing 'A Million Dreams' from *The Greatest Showman* with your already cracked iPhone for a microphone.

Deep breaths only get you so far. But you have to find a way to locate the chill in life, even when your patience is boiling over like that pasta you left on the hotplate for dinner. That's because this Chinese proverb is true. Hot, hot anger does nothing but harden a child's heart and toughen their skin.

'Cooking' is still needed. Certain behaviours must be discouraged, with both parents manning the ideal temperature for the best outcome. But tenderness is achieved through a low, steady, consistent heat, more than with random bursts of a burning flame.

Watch your temper, Dad.

79% of new dads agree
they need to 'be the rock'
for their family.

TO BE IN YOUR KIDS' MEMORIES TOMORROW

YOU HAVE TO BE IN THEIR LIVES TODAY

DADDY'S LITTLE GIRL

Madonna King

Mother of two

Journalist / Media commentator
Author of nine books including *Fathers and Daughters* and *Being 14*

Dads have never had a greater
opportunity to be more present
in their children's lives, and
to build solid, independent
connections with their daughters.
Whether it's a milkshake or a cup
of coffee on the way to school,
that one-on-one connection
is vital because it allows her to
know that Dad is there, for her.
Then, when she reaches
adolescence and tries to take
a step back, that connection keeps
the bond, however tricky, alive.

"Dads willing to demonstrate vulnerability are repaid with daughters who will open up to them."

I interviewed 1300 girls and 400 dads for my book *Fathers and Daughters*, along with dozens of school principals and teen psychologists and other experts. And I learned so much about the value of regular one-on-one connection with our daughters, and the importance of shared activities.

One dad loved AC/DC and instilled that love in his daughter. Together, they played their music too loud, and eventually flew from Perth to Sydney for a concert. My fifteen-year-old does pilates every Thursday night with her dad, my husband. A couple of weeks ago, I asked, 'What's the goss?' She winked at my husband, turned to me and said, 'Sorry, Mum, what goes on at pilates stays at pilates!'

It doesn't matter what they do together. What's important is that it is one-on-one with our daughter—or son. They know then they have an independent bond with their dad. They know he's got their back.

Quantity of time is not as important as quality. I'm a journalist—not a psychologist or an educator—but there is not an expert who disagrees with the fact that when dads are present, they really need to be present. It's that simple.

Dads willing to demonstrate vulnerability are repaid with daughters who will open up to them. Several teens said to me: 'Look, I wouldn't approach Dad over that, because he's never shown any fragility.' Separated families were a delightful exception because a girl, in her mid-teens, sees her dad's vulnerable side. Their dads will tell them that they 'stuffed up' or they are sorry their children have been put through a separation, or that they hadn't planned for their life to unravel in this way. And, for the girls, that's gold because then they know that Dad is not trying to be that all-being, all-knowing, all-strong, never-get-something-wrong sort of guy.

Madonna King

To the girls, this means they don't have to be perfect because Dad has admitted that he wasn't perfect. They can then tell their dads that they've made a mistake, or that they need advice . . . This is so important for fathers to know.

Dads too readily undervalue their role in dealing with their daughters in a practical way. Girls love five things about their dads: that they are rational, hard-working, successful, organised and calm. Those traits came up hundreds of time—so dads should never undervalue what they offer. One girl told me if she gets a C in maths, her dad asks whether she needs a tutor. 'Mum will just cry,' she said.

Another teen described it this way: 'Dad will stay out of the emotional stuff, and then he'll get a piece of paper, and he'll draw the problem in the middle. He won't make the decision for me, but he'll say, 'Well, these are your options.
1. Get new friends.
2. Go cold-turkey on social media.
3. Go back and confront them.'
Dads are really good at providing that practical advice and encouraging their kids to look for alternatives. They can still be the decision maker, but Dad is able to show them different paths.

Valuing their dad's opinion is more crucial than perhaps I understood when I started my research.

If a daughter comes home and says, 'I support a republic,' and Dad dismisses that as silly and immature, the hit to her self-belief is really strong. Girl after girl told me that, and it is the reason so many daughters stop sharing what they think with their parents.
'Why would I tell Dad something? He just dismisses it or says I'm wrong. So I just tell him what he thinks.' But if Dad says, 'Look, I disagree with your argument, but just explain to me your rationale,' that changes the discussion. She hears her father is interested. She might even go to school and ask her friends to help her work out her rationale!

The advice is that we should consider it a privilege that she is sharing her views, and testing out her values, with her father. He doesn't have to agree, and can oppose her argument—but the criticism should never relate to her. One principal of a big girls' school put it this way, and I just love this: 'Dads have to remember that they might be the QC in the courtroom, but they are always only Dad in the lounge room.'

"YOU ARE CONSTANTLY REMINDED OF WHAT YOUR OWN PARENTS MUST HAVE EXPERIENCED."

Guy Pearce

Father of Monte

Actor

INTERVIEW BY
Jenny Cooney / HFPA

When I started going out with Kate, who I was married to for twenty years, she told me, 'I don't want kids.' That was always fairly agreed between us.

But then I met my new partner, Carice, and she really wanted to have kids. I was never going to stop someone from having children, but it was this new consideration for me. And then I was reminded of how, when I was really, really young, I'd always liked the idea of having kids. So a lot of that came back to me.

I'm now old enough to feel like I can take on the responsibility of having a child. I mean, I've always been pretty responsible, but I was always really aware of the responsibility that having children involves. I have a sister with an intellectual disability who I've helped raise my entire life. So I didn't necessarily want to add a child to that. But then my sister is pretty self-sufficient now.

After having kids, you are constantly reminded of what your own parents must have experienced. When I look at this baby, I cannot help but realise on a much more visceral level that my mother looked at me like this, and my mother experienced me like this. I've had to learn how to change nappies and do all that sort of stuff as well, but I do think the realisation on a deeper level of what my parents have gone through hit me. I think all parents are grateful when their children start to realise that.

"I'm now old enough to feel like I can take on the responsibility of having a child."

TFH

THE OTHER HALF

"One of the greatest things a father can do for his children is to love their mother."

– Howard W. Hunter

You're working on your dad game, but don't lose sight of being a good husband, too.

Spot the odd one out:

- A bottle of red wine in a secluded booth at a dimly lit restaurant.
- A gentle stroll along a beach at dusk.
- A three-year-old with an earache and a runny nose.

Parenthood, it must be said, is not very conducive to romantic gestures. Saucy texts are replaced with desperate calls to pick up more baby formula. Dirty weekends are supplanted by kids' birthday parties. Date nights are postponed indefinitely when you're both so bone-tired you can barely speak.

Plus, as you'll have noticed from the stories in this book, we're in the middle of a bona fide revolution. More of our energy is devoted to our kids than ever before. By and large, this is a positive development. Unless your children then proceed to totally eclipse your relationship with your partner.

It turns out this hyper-focus on kids isn't too good for them either. David Code, author of *To Raise Happy Kids, Put Your Marriage First* (the clue's in the title here), warns that sacrificing your relationship for a child-centred existence can create demanding and entitled children. Being attentive parents is all very well, he suggests, but don't let it turn you into a lousy couple.

Some readjustment is, of course, inevitable in the marital-bliss department, so don't beat yourself up. No one has a perfect marriage and countless studies reveal that most relationships suffer after kids. Yet, at the same time, forewarned is forearmed.

Modern fatherhood is about making your own rules. Strive to avoid a moribund love-life by prioritising your partner ahead of your kids. Yes, it'll create a stronger family unit that will ultimately benefit them (as Hunter suggests). But more importantly, she's worth it, too.

**For those about to dad,
we salute you.**

DAVID BECKHAM IS STILL THE POSTER-BOY FOR MODERN FATHERHOOD

David Beckham

Father of Brooklyn, Romeo, Cruz and Harper Seven

Ex-footballer / Sports ambassador / Businessman / Icon

INTERVIEW BY
Luke Benedictus

Unexpectedly, David Beckham materialises through the back door and catches everyone in the hotel by surprise. He's dressed all in black—cashmere knit, slim-fit jeans, hi-top sneakers—with a TUDOR watch dangling from his tattooed wrist. For a couple of seconds, the room stops.

Perhaps it's the suddenness of his entrance that forces people to take a moment to regain their composure. More likely, it's the fact that meeting David Beckham is a bit weird. In person, the glare of his hyper-celebrity makes you blink. His face is so familiar, thanks to the goal celebrations, magazine covers and skyscraper-sized billboards, that your brain instinctively registers him as an old mate. Then you realise, of course, you've never actually met before and you're beaming at him in a slightly deranged way.

Those who've spent time with Beckham tend to say two things. The first is that he's just as pleasant as he appears in public. This, it transpires, is boring but true. The photographer has already recounted how, at a soccer clinic that morning, Beckham happily stood in the hot sun for way longer than official duties required to make sure every single kid (and then all their parents, too) got their precious selfies. Now there are yet more photos. But Beckham submits to the process with easy humour, flashing his bashful grin on cue.

The second truism about Beckham is that he's even better looking in the flesh. Infuriatingly, I can vouch for this, too. At forty-three, he's still lean and athletic, while beneath the furrowed brow and facial scruff his features combine that sure-fire blend of cragginess and preposterous symmetry.

Those looks certainly haven't hampered Beckham's status as a style icon and fixture on the best-dressed man lists. But what he's increasingly known for today is being the poster-boy for modern fatherhood. With four kids ranging in age from seven to nineteen, Beckham has become the paragon of the 21st century dad.

He's not just a modern dad because of his hands-on involvement—although he loves doing the school runs and cooking their meals (smoothies are his secret nutritional weapon, he tells me, 'because you can make a strawberry smoothie and then smuggle in vegetables without the kids even noticing').

Beckham's not only a modern dad because of the way he continues to look after himself, proving fatherhood needn't mean a slide into physical disrepair and trousers with elasticated waistbands. Or because of the fashionably 'creative' monikers he's bestowed on Harper Seven, Cruz, Romeo and Brooklyn.

No, the reason Beckham is the standard-bearer for the contemporary dad is far simpler: it all stems from his giddy devotion to his kids. He refers to his children as 'my motivation', and has been quoted as saying that leaving them can make him feel 'physically ill'.

> "He refers to his children as 'my motivation' and has been quoted as saying that leaving them can make him feel 'physically ill'."

A cursory scroll through his Instagram feed (55 million followers and counting) suggests that these are not empty words. Check the photo of him proudly posing by a newly assembled LEGO castle ('1am done . . . Someone's gonna have a nice surprise in the morning.') Or in that heart-melting clip of Beckham reduced to tears on his birthday as he embraces Brooklyn, who's unexpectedly returned from overseas to surprise his dad. (Being physically affectionate and in touch with his emotions wins him another big tick in the modern-dad stakes).

It's not as if he's in the goofy-grinned honeymoon period of dad life either. After all, Beckham became a father almost two decades ago, when he was twenty-three. 'Obviously, Victoria and I had Brooklyn at a very young age, but I always wanted that, because I wanted my kids to live through my career with me— through the highs, and obviously a couple of lows along the way. I always wanted that.'

He goes on to explain, 'I think you mature quicker with kids. You have more important things in life to worry about than your everyday worries, and life becomes all about the kids. I think that's what you learn as a father: you become less important and it's all about your children.'

Beckham also has a close relationship with his own dad. Ted Beckham was an Essex heating engineer who installed domestic boilers for a living. An avid Manchester United fan and frustrated player himself, Ted was determined to help David realise his own dreams, and he helped mastermind his son's footballing career. By the time David was a toddler, Ted was already making him balls to kick out of rolled-up socks. That support paid off when Beckham signed for United as a schoolboy.

"Never give up, no matter what." That was one of the things that my dad would always say to me,' Beckham says. 'If I got a kick in a game, I'd look over to him and he'd be like, "Get up! Get up! Don't show people that you're hurt!" There was a steeliness that he kind of instilled into me. It actually made me stronger as a person.'

"Your kids are always watching (always watching) and your conduct defines their values. If you want to teach your kids that hard work breeds success then Beckham's suggestion is you must step up to the plate yourself."

David Beckham

Yet Beckham's true legacy from his parents wasn't old-school grit but a boundless capacity for hard work. Today, at the age of seventy, his father still beavers away as a self-employed gas fitter. 'He still wants to work,' Beckham says.

'When we were kids he used to go out to work at six o'clock in the morning and often come home at nine o'clock at night. My mum was the same—she used to work during the day and then in the evenings, once my sisters and I were in bed, she'd do hairdressing until 12 o'clock at night.'

Therein lies the wellspring of Beckham's success. This tends to get lost amid the hysterical glitz that surrounds him—the model looks, the popstar-cum-fashion-designer wife, the showbiz hobbies (in his downtime Beckham rides motorbikes with Tom Cruise etc.). But Beckham's career as a footballer was always based on a formidable work ethic.

As a stick-thin youngster coming through the ranks, Beckham was never the most naturally gifted. So he ran harder instead. He consequently built up incredible stamina, and he remains one of the few athletes to have completed every level of the notorious beep test. To make up for his lack of technical flair, Beckham practised like a loon. Every day after training, he'd stay behind to work on those curling free-kicks that would become his match-winning trademark. The upshot: Beckham transformed his right boot into one of world football's most devastating weapons.

Sure, he was flamboyantly metrosexual and sported literally every haircut known to mankind (Mohican? Tick. Cornrows? Tick . . .), but as a player, he relied more on work-rate than razzle-dazzle—a true team player who'd sweat buckets for his team. Luis Figo, the former World Player of the Year and Becks' Real Madrid teammate summed things up: 'The image he has is totally different to what he is really like as a player and a person.'

And here lies the dilemma for Beckham as a father. His playing career at United, Real Madrid, LA Galaxy, AC Milan and Paris Saint Germain was phenomenally successful. At United alone he notched up six Premier League titles, two FA Cups and the Champions League. On the international stage, he played 115 times for England and captained his country fifty-nine times. Since then, Beckham has become a walking super-brand, amassing a personal fortune estimated at around £300 million. Beckham is the working-class boy who slogged his way up to conquer the world.

His astounding success means that Beckham's children enjoy an upbringing that's very different from his own. Their lives can indeed often look like something out of a '90s hip-hop video. His eldest son, Brooklyn, for example, boasts Elton John as a godfather and 11.5 million Instagram followers and, at the age of just seventeen, was hand-picked to photograph the ad campaign for the Burberry Brit fragrance.

All this raises a quandary that Beckham is acutely mindful of. How do you instil hunger and drive in kids who've had the keys to life handed to them on a gilt-edged plate? It's a question that Beckham has pondered deeply and the answer, for him, lies in his role as a dad.

'I still learn from my parents, I still watch them, they still guide me,' he says. 'And I've tried to do the same with my children. Because they do have a different upbringing to what I had, but the work ethic still has to come from the parents.'

That's why David Beckham continues to grind away, chasing down business interests with the same determination that he displayed on the pitch. He's jumped on a merry-go-round of endorsements and sponsorship deals: fragrances, fashion lines, watches, whiskey, and he continues to pursue new opportunities. He's in Australia to help AIA promote its campaign for healthier living. His latest business venture involves heading the ownership group for the new MLS soccer team in Miami that's due to make its debut in the 2020 season. Meanwhile, as a philanthropist, he's started the David Beckham 7 Fund with UNICEF to help the world's most vulnerable children.

Beckham does all this despite pocketing a rumoured £40,000-a-day over the past two years from the commercialisation of his brand. Why does he continue to hustle? It's because he's determined to send the right message to his kids.

'The reason I finished my (football) career at thirty-eight years old and continue to work as hard as I do now is because I want to set the right example,' Beckham says. 'I want to show my kids that now, after the first part of Dad's life and the first part of his career, he still continues to work hard. That's what I want them to learn.'

It's a principle that doesn't only apply to the ludicrously wealthy. You want to be a better dad? Beckham's advice would be to take a good look in the mirror and work on trying to become a better man. Your kids are always watching (always watching) and your conduct defines their values. If you want to teach your kids that hard work breeds success then Beckham's suggestion is you must step up to the plate yourself.

How then does the poster-boy for modern fatherhood want to be remembered as a dad? Beckham shrugs and gives that little half smile that makes every woman in the room inwardly swoon. 'Just as a hard-working father that loved his kids and would do anything for them.'

"I want to show my kids that now, after the first part of Dad's life and the first part of his career, he still continues to work hard. That's what I want them to learn."

89% of new fathers 'find real joy' in their role as a dad.

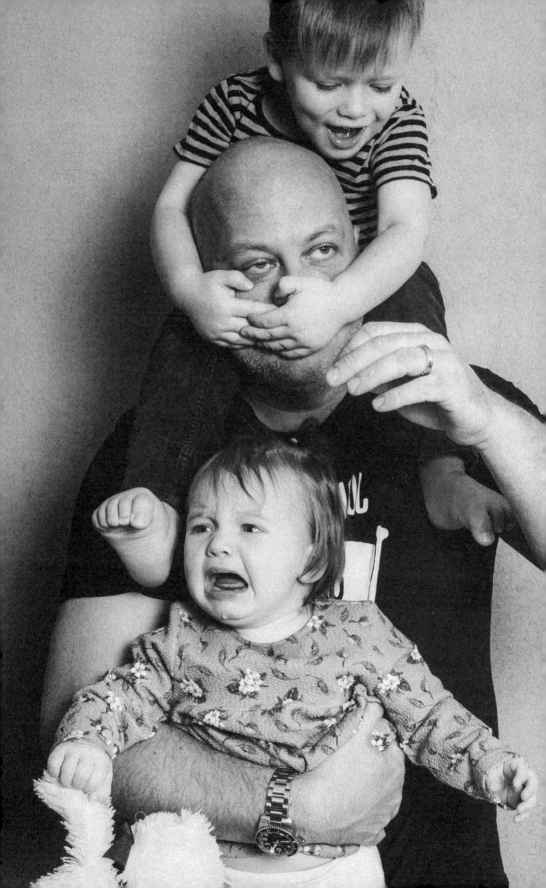

UPS AND DOWNS

"Raising children is terribly hard work, often thankless and mind-numbing, and yet the most rapturous experience available to adults."

— Andrew Solomon

Your emotional engine is about to be cranked into overdrive.

In just one sentence, Solomon is able to neatly package the great paradox of fatherhood. Because, let's be honest, there are days when looking after small kids can feel like the fate bestowed on Sisyphus, the king in Greek mythology forced to push a boulder up a steep hill for all eternity, only to watch it roll back down each time it came agonisingly close to the summit. Every father has experienced similar moments of defeat—times when parenting seems laborious, exhausting and bleak. And yet . . .

While Solomon's words acknowledge this incontestable fact, they also reflect the flipside. And he writes with genuine authority here, too.

This quote comes from Solomon's remarkable book *Far From the Tree*, in which he interviews more than 300 families with 'exceptional' children who live with a range of conditions, from autism and schizophrenia to severe multiple disabilities. It's fair to say these parents have a hell of a lot to contend with.

Yet what shines through these stories is the heroism of the parents. They display miraculous acceptance, bottomless love, and even gratitude for the often desperate experiences they must cope with, because that is the reality of who their kids are and it's what engaging with their child demands.

What Solomon's book illuminates is the boundless humanity that the parental role can unlock. Plus, it affirms the fundamental truth of fatherhood: you'll never regret having kids.

Emperor penguin dads

Stay together in a huddle to thwart brutal winter winds

With a solitary egg perched on their feet, they stand guard while the mothers hunt the ocean

Going without food for up to 115 days

Nature is constantly evolving

So are dads

THE DADS OF TOMORROW

Tom Harkin

Father of River

Workshop facilitator and personal development
expert for Tomorrow Architects and Tomorrow Man

My dream for dads of tomorrow is that they get to enjoy their whole life. The thing that kills me most about the narrow version of masculinity that we've had in the past, and something that still persists with a lot of blokes today, is that it results in men who are kind of dead inside. You've got all these grumpy old men who don't dance, they don't shed a tear, they don't celebrate, and they don't smile a whole lot. So much of a bloke's personality and experience is robbed from him when he has a narrow version of masculinity.

TFH

I grew up in a working-class town, Frankston, and men there don't dance. I moved to the city, and I learned how to rock a dance floor and let loose on a Saturday night. When I went back for my ten-year school reunion, I was the only bloke on the dance floor. It was sad. I'm out there rocking it with all the girls having a great time and I look around and there's literally a ring of blokes standing around, only able to tap their toes and hold their beer and have a pretty basic conversation with the guy next to them.

There's more life to be lived for the man of tomorrow and the father of tomorrow.

We know the world is changing faster and faster, and this is presenting us with new challenges. We've got this opportunity now, as men, to step up and lead the way in creating what the new man looks like.

The new man can connect with his kids. He can love them, hug and kiss them, and have really meaningful, deep conversations with them about their ups and downs. He doesn't need to be the silent, stoic bloke in the corner who just grunts and provides the money.

I'm looking forward to seeing guys embracing those so-called 'feminine' traits, but in a masculine form. Being able to let the tears roll down their cheek and not wipe them away. To be able to push through a tough conversation—talking with shaky voice and heart thumping—about the things that you're struggling with and need help with.

"Life's too short to be stiff and lonely and not be able to express yourself or express affection for those you love, or for them to know that you care about them."

Tom Harkin

It's so much more exciting than the alternative, and it doesn't need to look emasculating. It can look very masculine.

There is a myth that when a man talks about emotionally weighty issues, he comes across like a woman. It's not true. For Tomorrow Man, we work around the country with men of all ages—the hardest blokes in Australia—and when a man talks honestly about his emotions, it looks like a man talking honestly with emotion. It doesn't look like a woman. It's charismatic, it's really powerful and other blokes unanimously respect it.

For a long time, women have had this battle cry: 'We want it all. We don't want to just be at home!' I think guys now have that opportunity to also say, 'We want it all.' You can blitz it at work and go hard when you're doing that, but doing that shouldn't rob you of having a meaningful emotional connection with your son, your daughter or your wife or husband, or whoever you want to connect with.

Whether that means crying tears because your daughter's getting married, or welling up because your kid has just done something remarkable, or whether that's just you sitting in your lounge room looking at your child going, 'I love you so much and it's making me emotional.' That's fine. It's awesome. Because you're alive and in love.

Maybe it means you're able to rock the dance floor and have more fun, or to let loose and not feel like that might be stupid. Something that pisses me off so much is that the rules that we set up for young blokes often rob them of so many experiences. You end up with grumpy old men who didn't need to be that way. They could be getting so much more out of life.

When you go to countries that do have a more expansive version of masculinity, you see grown men dancing down the street, arm-in-arm, hand-in-hand, hugging each other, laughing. Life's too short to be stiff and lonely and not be able to express yourself or express affection for those you love, or for them to know that you care about them.

"There's more life to be lived for the man of tomorrow and the father of tomorrow."

It's such a crying shame that one of the only times some men get to shed a tear is when they're expressing high emotions, like when their team wins the Grand Final, when they're victorious. Because when you lock out the low emotions, like vulnerability and just admitting that you're struggling, if you clog that up, you also rob yourself of so many more of the highs. I think a lot of people don't understand that. When you lose the lows, you also lose the highs.

So, in some ways, I think we've got to man up. Let's not live within this bullshit limiting stereotype that we didn't write. Let's not miss out. Let's not hold on tight and fearfully to an old model of masculinity and throw our toys out of the cot because we're pissed off that things are changing. Things are changing and there's no going back.

We've got an opportunity here to decide, what does the man of tomorrow look like? And what does the dad of tomorrow look like? Let's discover it. Let's be pioneers. Let's step up and own this rather than being dragged into it. Let's grab some of that great stuff back.

Tom Harkin

When my son, River, is grown up, I hope he's able to reflect on a dad who was there for him, physically and emotionally. A dad who experiences a really full life.

I hope that he feels genuine love and respect for me. I hope he looks at me and thinks, 'I love you, Dad, because you have that connection with me.'

I hope that he looks at me and says, 'Thank you for having the courage to let me be my own man, but also thank you for giving me an example that gave me a foundation to start me on my way to discovering the man that I wanted to be.'

I hope that he looks at me and thinks, *I want to hang out with you, but also want your advice. I want your guidance. I want your ear. And I want you to listen to me.*

I hope he looks at me and thinks, *I'm so proud of what my dad has done. And I want to emulate and extend on the mark he's made.*

And I hope he enjoys me, rather than fears me or longs for my approval, or yearns for a connection with me. I've met so many men across the country, young and old, that feel so starved of their old man's love, connection and affirmation.

And I really want River to say, 'Yeah I know my dad loves me and thinks the world of me. I know he'll tell me honestly when he thinks I'm out of line or doing something that's not great for myself or the people around me. But I have a genuine connection with him. I know that he approves of me and loves me. And I admire his efforts to write a new way.'

That's what I hope for the dad of tomorrow, including me.

You are Dad. Hands on. Always on.

Interview

Paul Roos

Father of Dylan and Tyler

AFL legend / Premiership-winning coach
of the Sydney Swans / 2008 Australian Father
of the Year

Dylan Roos

Son and aspiring father

FATHER
AND
SON

"When I was his age, I thought I knew what my role was. You go to work, be tough, play sport. It was pretty defined."

– Paul Roos

Dylan   Your number one value? Everything you do is for family. You don't really do anything else. You have no other driving force.

Paul   I have you and Tyler. I have Tami, yes, but I have some friends.

Dylan   He has no friends. He has three friends. He has John. Rossy. One more?

Paul   Steveo.

Dylan   Steveo! Those are your three friends.

Paul   There's also Lynchy, and all my old footy buddies. But I think what Dylan's saying is right. I would generally prefer to spend time with my family than with anyone else. That is 100 per cent. I could say that without any fear of contradiction. If someone said, 'Roosy, do you want to come to the pub, or play golf or whatever' . . . Not that I didn't like doing other stuff, but I'd always say, 'Dylan, what are you doing today?' If the kids were busy, then I'd go and play golf.

Dylan   It's always been like that. When I was growing up, Dad was always there. He was never not there. He'd be playing in Perth on a Saturday, catch the red-eye flight at midnight and be there at my game at eight on Sunday morning. That was huge. That's something that you probably don't notice as much at the time as you do looking back.

I expected him to be there. I didn't know any different. I didn't realise that was something that most dads probably wouldn't have done. During primary school we also had a weekly breakfast at a cafe that was never cancelled; it was Thursday morning before school, every week with my mum and my brother. There are sensory memories— the smell of coffee and the noises of a cafe. I remember we used to play maths games, and we used to see how far we could double the numbers. I'd start at two, and go, 'Two, four, eight, sixteen, thirty-two, sixty-four, 128,' and I'd see how far I could go each time.

TFH

Dylan   I think you have to get some of the dad things right from the get-go, because you don't get the time back. But also because the time that your kids are the most malleable is when you're younger. Zero to seven are the formative years, when you're pretty much going to learn everything you are about from your parents, and after that, good luck!

Paul   My dad was different with us. It was just a different time. We would do things together, but separately, if you know what I mean. We would play at the same tennis club, but I was in a different tennis team. Dad was president of the club, and on the board of the primary school and Beverly Hills footy club, whereas I was probably more hands-on. I would coach my kids, or I would play tennis with them. My dad was around us kids, but I was with mine. I was just more inside the family rather than part of the family, if that makes sense.

My biggest challenge as a dad has been with words, rather than actions. I think my actions with Dylan are really good, but I'm not always good with words. My mum and dad split up when I was twenty. Dad got remarried and had this sort of different life after us. It wasn't like we didn't get on; we always got on really well. We just didn't have conversations.

I think Dylan will be a more engaged father in terms of vulnerability, and definitely in terms of communication, which I think is what we need. That conversation around males is changing, but it also makes it harder in a way. When I was his age, I thought I knew what my role was. You go to work, be tough, play sport. It was pretty defined.

Dylan   The other day I was just sitting at a cafe with one of my mates, and we were talking about how we were soulmates, and our thoughts around that. Correct me if I'm wrong, but you and your mates would never sit post-game of footie, talking about soulmates. So, I think we're levelling up in terms of our emotional intelligence.

Paul and Dylan Roos

Paul	I think that's the level of conversation that you'd love this next generation to have. The pub talk is not about sport. Sport's part of it, but the pub talk, the coffee talk is more around, 'How are you going as a dad? How are you going as a bloke? How are you going as a mate?' Getting underneath those conversations.
Dylan	Dad has said a couple of times that he hopes he raises two men to be better than he was. I hope that as well. As much as I love and respect my dad, I hope I'm a better father than him. Not because he was a bad father, but because you want to learn from your own experiences as a kid and then improve upon them.
Paul	I hope he's equally as family-oriented, equally as honest. I think some of the things he's talking about today are great.
Dylan	What you realise as you get older is that your parents are people, too. They make mistakes and you have to forgive them for the mistakes they've made, because there's no blueprint for being a parent. That will probably become a lot clearer when I have kids. If you can admit your mistakes to your kids, they're probably going to forgive you.

"When I was growing up, dad was always there."

– Dylan Roos

THE ADDITION POSITION

"Both parents have known someone the children have never known."

– Graham Greene

Having kids will change your life forever, but it will also enrich it.

Fatherhood triggers a radical shift in your identity. And it's largely a change for the better. But what Greene is hinting at here is the collateral impact of parenthood: it can obliterate your former sense of self.

When your personal freedom is buried under an avalanche of family duties, the dad role can suddenly take over. That's understandable—you want to step up to the task. Just don't let fatherhood erase all trace of your previous existence.

Maybe you were a runner in your child-free days, or you went to gigs, read novels or surfed. Sure, you'll have to scale things back a bit—sacrifice is part of the dad deal—but strive to keep some form of your passions alive. Don't fall prey to the one-dimensional life.

Dodging that fate is a challenge. It requires ongoing effort and teamwork with your partner, probably a decent babysitter, too. But keep shuffling the pieces until they click into place. If you can wangle some balance, it'll keep everything steadier. Your kids don't only have to replace things in your life. If you work it out right, they can actually prove the ultimate addition.

192 – The number of times you'll be interrupted on the toilet by your kid before they turn four.

CATCH UP WITH YOUR MATES; IT'S GOOD FOR YOU

Paul Villanti

Father of Michael and Louise

Executive Director Programs, Movember Foundation

"We found that spending time with mates helped dads stay resilient during those chaotic early days of parenting, when you're still trying to find your feet."

Babies change everything. Everything becomes bigger, brighter, louder and more heightened—the ups, and sometimes the downs. Any parent will tell you that while it's one of the toughest challenges you'll face, it's also the most rewarding.

Parenthood is a huge life change for both mums and dads but, until recently, it hasn't been acknowledged just how challenging those early months can be for new fathers.

Movember Foundation has worked with thousands of men over the years, and we know that fatherhood is one of the key transition points in life, when men become more likely to suffer from poor mental health.

Twice as many men become depressed in the first year after becoming a dad than that of the general population. That's why supporting new dads through this major life transition is a key priority for Movember.

We know that one of the factors that can really help dads adjust during this time of huge change is having close male friends to talk things through with.

Your dad mates are the ones who will really understand the big changes that being a parent brings. They get why you can't drop everything and come to the pub with fifteen minutes notice anymore. Or why the idea of an all-night poker game isn't that appealing. They understand what it's like to get up every hour with a baby who doesn't sleep. And they are the ones who you can ask the dumb questions that you're afraid to ask anyone else.

Having a friend you can turn to, who has been through the same situation and can tell you to hang in there, can really help you through the tough times.

They also know what it's like being the only dad at the playgroup or being called the 'babysitter' when you're simply looking after your own kid.

Friendships are a vital part of a healthy life—for both men and women. The Harvard Adult Development Study shows that relationships have the biggest influence on our long-term health and wellbeing. Having people to rely on keeps your brain healthier and reduces both emotional and physical pain.

Paul Villanti

When we invested in the Healthy Dads Initiative, through Beyond Blue, back in 2014, we discovered that spending time with mates helped dads stay resilient during those chaotic early days of parenting, when you're still trying to find your feet.

That's why we encourage guys to make a conscious and consistent effort to spend time with their old friends, as well as finding ways of making new ones. It's always good to start with something you already like doing. Whether that's cycling, going to the footy, surfing, brewing beer or fixing cars, you're more likely to form and maintain strong friendships with blokes that you have something in common with, doing something that you really like doing.

Taking a few hours' break from family life to catch up with your friends isn't selfish. It allows you to disconnect from everyday pressures, have a laugh, recharge your batteries and realise you're not the only guy in the trenches.

I have an annual camping trip that I go on with some close mates. Not only is this a way for me to stay tight with these great mates and spend a good amount of time together, but our kids are now at an age where they also enjoy being part of it.

"Taking a few hours break from family life to catch up with your friends isn't selfish. It allows you to disconnect from everyday pressures."

It's not easy to find the time to see your mates, but it's time well spent, not just for you but also for your relationship with your partner and your kids.

Ultimately, that'll make you a happier and healthier man—and that will make you a better dad, too.

TFH

2920 – The number of times you'll try to make your child laugh before they turn four.

"SO MANY MEN TELL ME THEY WISH THEY'D SPENT MORE TIME WITH THEIR KIDS."

Professor Bruce Robinson

Father of Simon, Scott and Amy

Leading cancer researcher / Founder of The Fathering Project

I've had to break the bad news to men who've got lung cancer. I've had to do it hundreds of times. Sometimes I have to tell men, who are sitting there with their partner, that their cancer is incurable— that they've only got six months to live.

Their reaction varies a lot. Most blokes are philosophical—they're aware they have a shadow on their lung so they're ready for the news. Other times, they can get upset. They may or may not cry, although their partner usually does.

If they mention regrets, they're nearly always the same. I've had so many men tell me they wish they'd spent more time with their kids, more time with their families. But what happened was they got too sucked into their work.

> "Men are increasingly aware that they're not just the icing on the cake; they are fundamental to their children's lives."

At first, I was thinking about how to help dads, but then the focus became more about kids. Because there's a great deal of research that shows that there's a strong link between good fathering and the reduction of the risks that kids face when it comes to drug abuse, alcohol, mental health and violence. The more involved a father is in his children's lives, the more likely they are to grow up happy and healthy.

We found that the most powerful untapped force for helping kids was to improve fathering. So the Fathering Project grew out of that. We started almost twenty years ago, and I think that men's attitudes to fatherhood have changed since then. Men are increasingly aware of just how important dads are. They're aware that they're not just the icing on the cake; they are fundamental to their children's lives. The young dads I work with now, they want to spend time with their families, much more so than back in the days when I was a young doctor.

Prof. Bruce Robinson

"The more involved a father is in his children's lives, the more likely they are to grow up happy and healthy."

But what's the good of knowing that you're important and then feeling guilty? At the Fathering Project we share road-tested ideas that dads can actually use to positively engage with their kids. What's a good one? Start organising 'dad dates'—regular occasions when you spend one-on-one time with your child. If you have three kids, you'll organise three different dates. It's all about making the opportunity to talk with and listen to your kids.

Right now, it's a good time to be a dad. When I was having children, there were no fathering groups— you'd just ask your wife. Now there's so much more knowledge and information that can help you be a better dad.

Today, I'm a grandparent. I watch my sons and see that they do a lot of the things with their kids that I did with them. They're committed dads, and that's partly because if you've had one yourself then you intuitively know what to do. Fathering is so much harder if you've had no role model. That's why being a good dad can affect not just your kids, but generations to come. I watch my sons being good dads with their children and I'm proud of them.

"Fathering is so much harder if you've had no role model."

TFH

BECAUSE DADS ARE BORN TOO

One day you become a father.
From that day, you will never
stop being one.

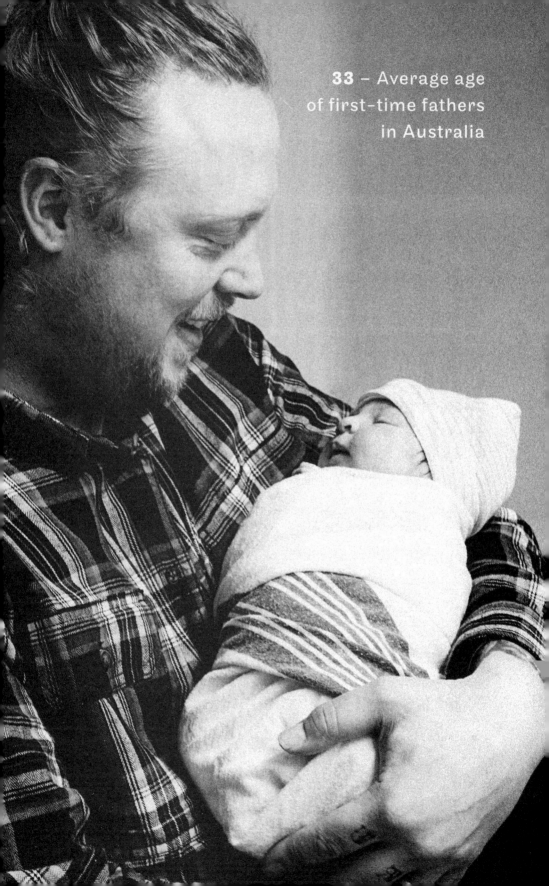

33 – Average age
of first–time fathers
in Australia

"GOLDIE AND I LOOK AT EACH OTHER ONCE IN A WHILE AND WE SAY, 'WELL, WE DID PRETTY GOOD THERE.'"

Kurt Russell

Father of Boston, Wyatt, Oliver and Kate

Actor

INTERVIEW BY
Jenny Cooney / HFPA

I guess we all grow up. And as we get older and begin to look at having families of our own, we try to imitate the good things about our original family as best we can.

That's an interesting double-edged sword because, while you can try to repeat the good things about your upbringing, this can also be a trap. Because if the people that you're trying to create all that for don't come from that, well, then you can often find yourself butting heads and trying to make something happen that can never happen.

Kurt Russell

So you have to walk that fine line between doing what you think is right and what they see as right. And it's a daily choice, right? It's a daily choice.

It always mattered to me; my family always mattered. I felt that with the decisions that I was making as a dad, I wanted to present a picture of family for my children that was positive, and something that they would maybe want to emulate as well. You get overzealous at times, and sometimes you get it just right.

I'm very proud of my kids because I think they're really nice people. I have these four people who I love spending time with—being with them is my favourite thing to do. I'm really fortunate that way. Goldie and I look at each other once in a while and we say, 'Well, we did pretty good there.' Usually it's after considering some other things we didn't do so well. And it's just about that time that something bad will happen, I guess.

But so far we've been really fortunate in the children that we had. They have always been fun to be around, and it's been fun to be a part of what's going on in their lives.

I guess the movie that I put in my head about what I wanted my life to look like came about, for the most part, because it happened with Goldie, and also because of the way each and every one of my children turned out to be. I was fortunate. Whether I'm one of the reasons for that I have no idea. But as long as I feel that they're enjoying life and they're having a good time, well, that's all I ever wanted.

"It always mattered to me; my family always mattered."

RESISTANCE IS FUTILE

"At sixteen, you still think you can escape from your father . . . You don't hear his whisper in your blood."

– Salman Rushdie

It's hard to pull a fast one on your genetic fate.

It's a moment that can catapult you headlong into a brutal midlife crisis.

You're sat at the kitchen table, idly scanning the sports pages and plotting the weekend ahead. What'll you do after dropping the kids off for swimming lessons, you wonder. Maybe stop by Bunnings to buy a new strimmer for the lawn? Your mood brightens instantly at the prospect. And then it hits you: you've turned into your dad.

This is the stunning moment of clarity Rushdie is predicting. Long before we clock it, the words we speak, the gestures we make, even our facial features, are slowly transforming. Until, at last, the inevitable metamorphosis is not only complete, but undeniable.

In retrospect, all that teenage rebellion was a waste of time. Those poorly rolled joints and ill-advised piercings? They were all for nought. The tidal pull of your DNA or, as Rushdie puts it, 'his whisper in your blood' overrides such getaway efforts.

Where it gets really confronting is when your father's legacy starts to manifest itself physically. You look in the mirror and notice a familiar sharpening of the features, a gentle stoop about your shoulders.

The final transformation has begun. Hopefully, your dad's mantle is worth inheriting, and your relationship good enough that this generational melding doesn't seem so bad. If that's not the case, well, maybe focus on his positive traits and try to sidestep the bad as you strive to avoid his mistakes.

You owe it to your kids to at least give it a go. After all, in thirty years' time, they'll find themselves in the same situation—frowning into the mirror, seeing your ghost materialise from within. What'll you do between now and then to ensure that moment brings a smile not a wince?

THE WORST ADVICE I EVER GOT ABOUT FATHERHOOD

Luke Benedictus

Becoming a dad can feel like death by endless, helpful suggestions. But some advice is particularly dangerous.

'Remember, boys like simple names,' she said. 'And girls hate to have the same name as other girls in their class.'

This, you understand, wasn't the worst piece of advice I ever got about fatherhood. I even thought it was relatively sane. But that tip-off came from the same source as the bad advice that followed. She was an older woman at work—I'll call her Pam.

Now, I'd always got along with Pam. She was in her early fifties, with a mahogany perma-tan, peroxide white hair and a voice husky from a squillion cigarettes. She was like an older stateswoman of the office whose worldview flickered between irreverence and NSFW depravity. Maybe she was a little batty, but she was smart and funny, too.

I liked her.

Plus, she was also the most doting mum I'd ever met. Her work cubicle was like a shrine of maternal devotion. Every inch of wall space was plastered with a mad collage of photos of her long-haired son.

So when my (now) wife became pregnant, Pam took a real interest and occasionally slipped me nuggets of insider info from the other side. One afternoon in the kitchen, I got another impromptu pep talk. 'When you become a dad,' she said, 'the most important thing is to look after your wife, so she can look after the baby.'

I nodded and stashed the info away for future reference. This sounded like more solid intel.

What Pam was suggesting I do was make sure my wife's every waking need was taken care of. Freeing her from the domestic treadmill made sense, I thought, because naturally she'd have a more intuitive sense of the baby's needs. Effectively, it was a divide-and-conquer strategy in a newborn nappy-pack.

That piece of advice stayed with me. I was receptive to its message, I think, because your protective instincts blaze more fiercely after you've watched your wife endure the long grind of pregnancy and the blood-curdling craziness of childbirth. Witnessing that process only deepens your sense of conjugal obligation. Suddenly you're in total awe of your wife.

"As a dad, your role in childbirth is largely confined to that of hand-holder, cheerleader and compiler of really shit 'chill-out' playlists."

Luke Benedictus

The upshot is that, more than ever, you really want to take care of the mother of your child. So you cook batches of food for the freezer, amass a huge stockpile of nappies and uncover yet another source of emasculation as you struggle to install the rear-facing baby-seat (I was forced to seek professional help). You're now the default administrator of back-rubs and maker of endless cups of tea. Your role as father will be to protect and serve.

And that part of Pam's advice was fine. You absolutely should look after your wife. But that's the sneaky thing about booby-traps: on the surface they look innocuous, so you blunder onwards, then BOOM! In the hidden-danger stakes those words were the tree branches masking a pit filled with razor-sharp spikes. And I didn't get away unskewered.

'Look after your wife so that she can look after your baby.' It's the second bit that's problematic for a dad, and I only realise it now that I have a couple of kids under my belt. It's dangerous because it nudges you to withdraw from the engine room of parenthood, gently ushering you towards a more peripheral role. And you hardly need another push because multiple forces are edging you in that direction right from the off.

For starters, you can't circumnavigate the basic facts of human biology. Nature determines that the primary bond exists between mother and child. As a dad, your role in childbirth is largely confined to that of hand-holder, cheerleader and compiler of really shit 'chill-out' playlists. Whether or not you cut the cord, in the delivery room you're little more than a pillar of moral support with a frozen grin.

After that, a whirlwind of factors conspires to keep you in that auxiliary role. Emotionally, men can often be slightly distanced from the action. It's not uncommon for dads to experience a delay in bonding with their babies in the early stages. The paternal connection requires time and prolonged contact to develop.

Then there's the shit-fight over parental leave. In all but the most enlightened companies, the skimpy entitlements for new dads create another roadblock for the aspiring co-parent. After a couple of weeks in a shell-shocked daze, you're plonked back into the office while your partner is left on the sofa holding the baby.

TFH

And so it begins. Your partner's daily exposure to your child starts to build up her confidence and expertise. She learns how to read the baby's mood, soothe his frequent outbursts and lull him back to sleep. Before long she's turned into the household font of childcare know-how. As for you? Now you're Mum's assistant.

The roles are cast. Unsure what to feed the toddler for breakfast when the Rice Bubbles run out? Ask your wife. Can't stop the baby from wailing? Hand him over to her. Your wife has already turned into the go-to parent in all matters requiring emotional comfort or domestic nous.

There lies the trap. And it's so, so easy for things to play out this way. Subscribe to the view that it's your wife's responsibility to 'look after your baby' and it's already a done deal. Not a positive one, either. What you're sleepwalking into here is an act of subjugation that relegates you to a lesser parenting role while heaping more pressure onto your frazzled wife (who's probably doing most of the night-shift as you fall short in the boob department). You have to fight against this dynamic because it doesn't have to be this way.

Think for a second about what you do at work. Perhaps you're an entrepreneur or an engineer, a maths teacher or a mechanic. Whatever. Chances are that at some stage of your career trajectory your role required some degree of professional expertise. Today, you can handle technical complexity and the snake pit of office politics. You can seal a deal, schmooze clients and know just how much to kow-tow to your idiot boss.

The bottom line: you've got the skills to pay the bills. In which case, figuring out how to feed and bathe your children before getting them ready for bed is definitely not beyond your scope of capabilities. You can deal.

"Paternal confidence only comes from spending time in the saddle or, more specifically, the soft-play centre."

Luke Benedictus

And if you don't feel like you can yet, well, that's okay, too. But you can train up fast. Like everything in life from crosswords to corporate embezzlement, your dad-game will only get better with practise. Paternal confidence comes from spending time in the saddle or, more specifically, the soft-play centre. But, once you develop it, there's a huge pay-off there for you.

Most men are conditioned to define themselves by their jobs. Your profession becomes the bedrock of your identity. But that's a high-risk play in the self-worth stakes, especially in a work environment yet to get its head around automation and artificial intelligence, plus the usual suspects of takeovers, redundancies and trigger-happy execs. A job for life? That no longer exists.

Plus, unless you're a rock star or Scarlett Johansson's personal masseur, you have to ask yourself how much you really love your job. Was it your childhood dream to work in middle management? Or are you simply doing your best, like the rest of us, plugging away in an okay gig that puts food on the table and pays your eye-watering mortgage.

There's more to life than work. Taking that active role in your kids' lives can help you recalibrate, and maybe even strike a happier balance. Fatherhood isn't all sunshine and rainbows. Often, it's scary hailstorms or that specific type of nonstop drizzle that gradually wears away your last reserves of optimism. Being a dad can, at times, prove tiresome, frustrating and wretchedly dull. But then you get the moments of payback.

Right now, because fatherhood has taught me to multi-task, I'm writing this on my phone. My eight-month-old son, clad in just a sunhat and nappy, is finally sleeping (thank fuck!) on my chest in a papoose. We're sitting on a wall in the dappled shade of a plane tree just near Kings Cross. And at this precise moment, feeling his bodyweight slumped against me, everything feels right. Sure, life is a shit-storm right now. I've got two kids under two, my to-do list gives me palpitations and I'm moving interstate in two weeks.

Yet, sitting here right now, cradling my son's head in one hand . . . well, it not only calms me, but it gives me a sense of perspective. Frankly, there's nowhere I'd rather be, even if I was Scarlett Johansson's personal masseur.

TFH

EMBRACE
THE CHAOS

When did I last have sex?

How long does it take for us to simply leave the house?

Please, please go to sleep.

We have to go to how many birthday parties this weekend?

I need to start exercising again.

And drinking a bit less too.

Just go to fucking sleep!

Where's your other shoe?

What day is it again?

Where did you get that from?

Mustn't swear in front of the kids.

Put your sister down!

Shit! Stop drawing on the wall!

Who left that bastard piece of LEGO on the floor?

Don't swear in front of the kids.

"WE CAN REFRAME WHAT IT MEANS TO 'PROVIDE' FOR OUR FAMILIES."

Aladdin Jones

Father of Karuna and Mani

Counsellor and community facilitator

I do a lot of counselling and group-work with men and families, and part of this work is about supporting new dads. I recently spoke with a stay-at-home dad with an eighteen-month-old son. He spoke of his own father, a farmer who used to work flat-out seven days a week. 'I remember my dad played with me a few times,' he recalled. 'Once, we played with a tractor at Christmas.

'It wasn't that Dad didn't mean well, he just wasn't available,' he continued. 'He was so often exhausted and stressed about money.'

As a stay-at-home dad, this dad now has the day-to-day responsibility of looking after their young son. They're certainly playing with tractors far more often.

Many men over forty admit that when they were growing up they weren't close with their dad. But imagine if our children can say, 'Yeah, I know my dad well. He's really there for me' not just as they are growing up, but throughout their lives.

Things are starting to change. I'm seeing more new dads who have now developed skills that enable them to be present in their children's lives, and to model better communication with an adult partner. This is a real game-changer for the next generation. A connected dad is part of creating healthy relationships.

"Research shows that defining ourselves more broadly results in better mental health, better relationships, happier families."

Society has always told men that they're supposed to have all the answers: you're supposed to be strong, silent and not show your emotions. That has now changed. For the first time in history, we are presented with the opportunity to not be so constrained by what it is to 'be a man'. We can now live outside of the traditional 'man box' and not be restricted by such a narrow definition of masculinity. And research shows that defining ourselves more broadly results in better mental health, better relationships and happier families. Those are strong motivators to step up to the opportunity!

TFH

New dads are at the forefront of this change; they're the icebreakers redefining masculinity. They have the opportunity to be a key part of redefining gender roles and stereotypes by demonstrating vulnerability and openness in a way that previous generations never dreamed of. It's an exciting time to be alive and to be a dad.

Personally, I've been two types of dad: when my older daughter was still young, I was more of a stay-at-home dad. I was studying for the first few years of her life, while my wife, Tess, was 'the breadwinner' as a primary school teacher. During this period, there were the challenges of adjusting to parenthood and the steep learning curve of juggling responsibilities with endless infant needs. We'd go for long walks, or I'd take her swimming or to playgrounds where, more often than not, I'd be the only dad present. I absolutely loved that time, where I had the opportunity to simply be with my daughter, to be present.

Later, it changed. Our second daughter came along and I was working full-time and renovating an old house. I was also doing more studying, and had less time to be. In hindsight, the stress levels were high. In addition to the workload stress, at some point I felt like I was missing out on my daughters' lives. When I did have interactions

with them, or my partner, they weren't getting the best of me, they were getting a tired and stressed version. At the time, it felt like I was sacrificing myself to be a 'provider' for the family. While I can say that I was just doing what was needed, the fact is my family were only getting part of me. After a couple of health scares, I asked myself if it was worth it. The answer was no, so we changed things up again.

We can talk about gender equality, or we can actively pursue it. Now, Tess and I work about the same hours a week. That is, we both have part-time roles that are more local and flexible. We both earn about the same amount of money and we both do about the same amount on the home front. There's just that bit more space to be present, not just for the kids, but also for ourselves and our relationship. That model works well for us. Working flat-out brought in more money, but the cost to our health, our happiness and the quality of our relationships was pretty high.

Aladdin Jones

The older model of fatherhood was more about providing the money, putting food on the table and paying the mortgage. But if we step outside of that, we can reframe what it means to 'provide' for our families. This might mean taking the time to grow some vegetables together. Or, even better, it could mean providing emotional support. And what a provision that is!

This kind of emotional investment into children and relationships pays off hugely. It's good for dads to think in those terms. In the case of teenage girls, we know that when they have a father who is emotionally invested in them and physically present, they're more likely to have a better relationship with their own bodies, they're likely to have better mental health, and they're likely to seek out better relationships as they get older. This doesn't start when they are sixteen, it starts before they can say the word 'dad'.

In my work, I come across more and more dads who are saying, 'I just want to be at home. I feel like I'm missing out.' I think that's positive. And okay, it might not feel great to have that sense of missing out. But at some level these guys are connecting with a longing to be present with their family. And that's another sign of the great change that's happening.

There is no guidebook for this new type of dad, but we're having a go. This change isn't easy, but neither is being a father. It is the new generation who are driving this change, they're the ones having to learn new ways of doing things, while at the same time unlearning how things were done in the past.

But it's not about searching for the answers either. Every situation is unique, just like you are. It's more about dads learning to share their worlds. It's those shared moments of acknowledging, 'Yeah, geez, it's hard! And it's great!' In doing so, we can realise we're not alone in the sleepless nights, the fatigue, the relationship stresses and financial strains. But we're also not alone in experiencing all the good things that fatherhood brings, too.

"There's no guidebook for this new type of dad, but we're having a go."

What nobody tells you about fatherhood
Is that you can dad your way,
Without any experience,
Without any training,
And that's okay.
That's where
All the joy
Kicks in,
Hard.

You
Are the
First dad
In history to
Do it your way.
Your legacy starts now.

"YOU WANT TO MAKE SURE THAT YOU'RE CONSTANTLY EVOLVING."

David Campbell

Father of Leo, Billy and Betty

Singer / TV presenter

INTERVIEW BY
Luke Benedictus

I found out that my father was Jimmy Barnes when I was ten. Lightning struck that day for me; I was emotionally rocked to find out.

Not having that direct time with my father, especially in the formative years, has affected me greatly as a parent. I really want to make sure I am a strong presence in my children's lives. It's vitally important for me to be around. I want my kids to know that I'm here for them.

That's coming from a place of being extremely mindful that I didn't always have that, and knowing that I missed it. Dad and I are very close now, but being an entertainer's kid—it wasn't 'normal' parenting. I don't know how to fix a tyre or how to put up a shelf because I didn't have a father around who did what regular fathers did. That's just the way it was.

But what's more important than all of that practical dad stuff is that you're there emotionally for your kids. When I was around ten, my dad and his wife, Jane, came into my life, and I put them to the test a few times. But I soon knew, deep down, that they were emotionally committed to raising me, even from a distance. Jane always said, 'You are part of my family. You are not a stepson to me.' Even now, she hates it when I refer to her as a stepmother.

I don't know if I was an alcoholic, but I was definitely skirting around the edges. I was certainly a binge drinker.

David Campbell

I don't know if I was an alcoholic, but I was definitely skirting around the edges. I was certainly a binge drinker. I'd get on it with my mates and, because I was in a band and because of who my father was, I sort of fell into going hard at it.

As a parent, it was definitely not the right or the safe thing to do. That doesn't mean that my kids or my wife were ever unsafe with me. But emotionally, I sort of stared into this dark room and saw where it could all head. And I was very lucky to pull the ripcord and get out before it was all too late.

The turning point came when Lisa, my wife, and I were going on a holiday to Broome. The night before we went, we decided to have some drinks. I woke up the next morning, the day of the holiday, and I was sick as a dog. I was so hungover.

I had to pack quickly and get to the airport and I couldn't stop sweating—I felt so sick. I remember my son Leo, who was three-and-a-half, saying to Lisa, 'Dad's not feeling well.'

At that moment, this alarm bel just went off in my head. It was like, *No, that's not the memory you're going to have of me. You're not going to remember dad feeling sick on the weekend because he had another big night with his mates. You're not going to remember dad getting drunk every Saturday night.*

Because I grew up around that. I saw my dad struggle with addiction and I also saw the devastating impact that could have on children—knew the effect alcohol-related incidents in my family had had on me. I knew that that wasn't the way to parent. You don't want to put a child at risk of that.

On the way to Broome, I just slept until the plane landed and then I got in the pool and I started to feel better. We went to lunch and I said to Lisa, 'That's it. I'm done drinking.' A month later, Lisa joined me as well.

And it's the greatest relief I've ever felt. It's like putting down the heaviest load. I knew that my drinking was stopping me from being able to grow because it was numbing my feelings, so I didn't have to deal with them.

TFH

Since I gave up drinking, I've had to identify and confront a lot of things about myself that I couldn't before. I've realised that I grew up with a lot of shame and a lack of self-worth.

When you've had a very confused upbringing, and you're raised by a single parent and you realise that people have lied to you (and look, there are kids who have gone through much, much worse) . . . I think that did have an impact on my psyche and on my life.

For me to be able to deal with that, and in order for me to raise mindful and emotionally intelligent kids, I had to get out of my own way. I had to stop numbing myself and acting like it was okay, because it wasn't okay.

A lot of my challenges were down to my own anxiety. I was a highly anxious person, and that was going to get in the way of me raising a child. With a lot of therapy and self-analysis, I can deal with that aspect of my personality a bit more. But I couldn't do that when I was drinking because it just took the edge off. And I don't want to take the edge off. When it comes to my children and my wife, I really want to be clear with my intentions. I've seen the damage it does when you don't do that, and I don't want that. Somehow, I had to stop the cycle. So I did.

When I became a parent, I realised that I need to be mirroring what I want my kids to be. You obviously want your kids to be version 2.0 of you, but if the version that you're putting out there is rubbish, well, then they're just going to lap you in their teens.

David Campbell

"When I became a parent, I realised that I need to be mirroring what I want my kids to be."

You want to make sure that you're constantly evolving. I guess that's why I'm striving to do different things now by being sober, by eating a vegan diet and by getting more involved in what we're doing to the planet. It's all to do with my kids.

I started eating differently because I wanted to be healthier, but then that turned into something bigger: wanting to improve the planet for my kids and actively show them that you can make healthier choices and be more physically active.

My kids still eat a bit of meat. I'm not a zealot about it—I want them to make their own choices. But the example that Lisa and I try to set is one that I think is really important. Hopefully it helps my kids continue to make good choices in their lives.

So I look at myself and I try to be better. And a lot of that really is to do with Leo, Billy and Betty. I want them to never have to worry about their dad. I always want them to be able to trust who I am. And I want them to know that I started off as a bogan kid from Adelaide with way too much energy and a chip on his shoulder. I was highly anxious, and I used that energy to get on stage. But that wasn't me forever. I changed and grew into something else.

It's not like I'm Superman. I wake up every day and don't know if I'm going to have an anxiety attack or a panic attack. And I don't know if I'm going to make a bad decision that day or not. But what I do know is that I can reduce that risk by not drinking booze, by being conscious of how I eat and by spending conscious time with my kids where I'm not on my phone. Then I feel like I've done the right thing for that day, and that's all I can do.

TFH

"BIG HOUSES ARE CREATING DYSFUNCTIONAL FAMILY UNITS."

Peter Maddison

Father of Woody, Ruby and Finn

Architect / Presenter of *Grand Designs Australia*

TFH

Because of the size of many modern houses, the family unit is being eroded. You've got the basement theatre, where people can just go and lock themselves in a black room—no conversation.
The lights go down, you feel like you're in Gold Class, whoop-di-doo! And then you spend the whole evening sitting next to each other and not communicating!

These big houses are creating dysfunctional family units. There's no more standing around the sink doing the dishes at night. What a great thing that is, what a lost tradition that is!
My mum insisted that either my brother or I took it in turns at drying.
Then, enter the dishwasher, and now you can't even get the kids to unload or load the dishwasher. They're off in their own space in their Facebook world.

FIVE WAYS WE'RE SCREWING UP THE FAMILY FLOORPLAN

With the (terrible) open kitchen/family room

1

It's very much the thing of the day to have open plan, but, having a family myself, I know there are times where there's a need for the separation between the function of cooking and then the idea of living. Personally, I think the idea has hairs on it.

2

By ignoring acoustics

A family space is one where there's a lot of activity. I think this is lost in a lot of the spaces being created today. I'd be aware of the acoustic performance of a family space. Having had three children myself, I know what it's like to be in a noisy space; it's really wearing. In a lot of family houses there are big family rooms that have plasterboard ceilings and walls, timber floors, lots of floor to ceiling glass and it's like a bloody echo chamber. Nice big open room, interactive kitchen and living area but it's dysfunctional. There's a TV going in one corner, so the talk gets louder, then you get a few people in there and it becomes unintelligible. Never discount acoustics when planning a family space.

TFH

By building 'kids' retreats' and letting them disappear

3

Some people like to reproduce the living space for the kids, like a 'kids' retreat' and say, 'We'll do our own space downstairs and that way we can have flexibility.' Well, the kids will never come downstairs. There's no family interaction. They're on an intercom, 'Dinner's ready,' then 'Dinner's getting cold,' then 'Dinner's ready! Come downstairs you little rug rats!' That leads to segregation of family values. You're separating your living space from their living space and there's no interaction. That's not a healthy thing to have.

With too many TV zones

When there are four huge TV screens in the house, there's never any reason to come together to watch it as a family. Density breeds social values. You get to make eye contact with your kids, and you're forced to say something because you're passing by them, or sitting next to them on the couch. The reduced density within the family home is eroding the connectedness of families who are living together, apart.

Peter Maddison

By subscribing to the logic that a big house is good for families

5

It's the notion that you've got to have a house that's bigger than your parents had; in my generation, this was considered a mark of success. I know when I left my parents' house in Parkdale (Victoria) I thought, 'I can do better than them.' And I have. I've got a bigger house than they've got, but is it better?

I slept in a bedroom with my brother 'til I was fourteen, and I thought I never wanted to do that again. So there's this notion of upsizing that's hereditary, but that will change. It has to be bred out and I think that's coming. This discussion won't be had in our children's time; I think their generation will have different aspirations. Meanwhile, there's a 100 kilometre urban sprawl from east to west, and that will increase to 150 kilometres in our lifetime.

TFH

90% of dads say being a parent
is their greatest joy.

85% of dads say being
a father is the best job in the world.

73% of dads say their life
began when they became a dad.

TFH

WALK THE WALK

"Children have never been very good at listening to their elders, but they have never failed to imitate them."

– James Baldwin

Talk is cheap. When it comes to parenting, your kids will learn by example.

Talk about an inconvenient truth. Things would be so much easier if you could set your kids on the path to success just by doling out key life lessons at opportune moments ('Never wear a hat that's cooler than you are,' etc.).

Sadly, wise words alone won't cut it. What's instructive is how you lead your own life. The repercussions of this are far-reaching. That recent outburst, when you yelled at the taxi driver who swerved in front of you? Sure, he deserved that technicolour spray, but it wasn't too clever with both of your sons strapped into the backseat, particularly when studies reveal that men's driving styles are most influenced by their dads.

The demands of such round-the-clock vigilance are enough to make you reach for a drink. Except another irksome study claims that kids who regularly see their parents boozing are twice as likely to binge-drink themselves.

You get the idea. And Baldwin's practise-what-you-preach memo is especially true in your role as a dad. If you're an uncle, you can get away with being a good example or a cautionary tale. As a father, you have to at least try and model the right behaviour.

That's a mighty responsibility, but it also offers a rare chance to evolve. Fatherhood encourages you to step up and become more patient, more considerate and more reasonable. Having kids is the ultimate incentive to try and become a better man. Your self-development intensive starts now.

TFH

ON THE ROAD

Tristan White

At first, travelling for work can feel like a glamorous perk. You mop up frequent-flyer points, nab a good night's sleep in a hotel and (whisper it) also wangle a temporary break from the parenting treadmill. But when you've got a young family and you're away from home a lot, the novelty quickly wears thin. And being forced to buddy up with Trevor from sales is far from the only downside.

TFH

Researchers from the University of Surrey (UK) and Lund University (Sweden) found that frequent work trips can trigger an avalanche of health, social and family problems. The study called 'The dark side of hypermobility' reveals that business trips can lead to stress, loneliness and the fraying of family bonds. The partner at home often starts to feel abandoned and resentful, while the traveller experiences guilt at being away.

Tristan White has confronted these problems head-on. He's the founder and CEO of The Physio Co, a business that, for ten years straight, has ranked as one of Australia's 50 Best Places to Work. White built the company up from scratch and now employs 150 team members across five states. The sticking point? White is also the father to three young children: Alexandra (seven), Harriet (four) and Roman (two).

Reconciling these responsibilities is a real challenge. White's family are based in Foster on the Victorian coast, but three days a week he finds himself in Melbourne, Sydney, Adelaide, Brisbane or wherever he needs to be to lead the team.

The constant travel takes its toll. 'The hardest thing is not being there for my wife and kids,' White says. 'Not being physically present to help Kimberley with the inevitable challenges that happen with little ones—like the daily school and kinder drop-offs, toddler tantrums and illnesses is really tough. This is a time of life when it feels bloody hard.'

In a bid to tackle the problem, White and his wife, Kimberley, devised a simple ritual to maintain strong family connections. Whenever he's away for work, the whole family bookend each day with FaceTime chats at 6.45 a.m. and 6.45 p.m.

"When he was at home, my father was present. I have that memory of him being very invested."

Tristan White

'It's pretty hectic on that call, trying to talk to four people at a time,' White says. 'But each of the kids will take the phone in turn and we'll have a quick one-on-one where I can ask them what they're doing that day and how they're feeling about it.'

During the call, White will show his kids where he is, the view from his window and what he's up to (invariably work on his laptop). It's a basic process, but one that provides his kids with a welcome dose of attention, reassurance and routine.

'Sometimes we just eat Weet-Bix or Rice Bubbles together,' White says. 'It's just about connection.'

White admits it's not a foolproof tactic. His own mind-set, he explains, is crucial to its success. Whenever he's stressed or distracted, the chat with his kids is rarely effective: 'I have to show up engaged and connected or it just doesn't work.'

To further offset his weekly absences, White has organised his schedule so that he now works from home the other two days a week. 'When I'm at home, we eat dinner together each night,' he says. 'I do school and kinder drop-offs, coach Alex's under-tens basketball team and go to plenty of swimming lessons. I do my best to be as involved as possible.'

The situation echoes that of White's own father, who worked on the Bass Strait oil rigs. 'The nature of his work meant he'd be home for a week and then away for a week. But when he was at home, my father was present,' he recalls. 'I have that memory of him being very invested.'

For now, White doesn't pretend he's found a magic solution. The juggling act between business and family remains a work in progress, but he and his wife are happily married and at least working together on finding the counterbalance. This remains an ongoing challenge. 'We don't always get it right,' he says. 'Sometimes it works and sometimes it doesn't.'

To the unseen father,

Whose forehead bears the indentation
of the cot's rungs.

Pressed into them, he pats and pats,
and then rubs in a circular motion.

Then pats again.

Slowing, slowing—hand poised
above the baby's back,

He wonders if she will stir,

Only to have her wake as he leaves
the room on all fours.

Foiled by the squeak of the
bedroom door.

Her alarm, when it howls, is instantaneous
and full-bodied.

The unseen father returns to her
cot-side to begin the ritual again.

To the unseen father,

Who waits in the car outside the party.

Weighing up the pros and cons
of going in to find his daughter.

Are there even parents in there?

Will she be mortified? Should he
just text again?

Twenty minutes. Half an hour.

He opens the door and gets out,
only to see his daughter walking
towards the car.

In an outfit for a woman, not a girl.

'I can't believe you were going
to come in. Never do that.'

The unseen father, accustomed
to the abuse, smiles.

And breathes deeper.

His daughter is home safe.

TFH

THE ONLY JOB THAT REALLY COUNTS

"DIVORCE HAS, I FEEL, MADE ME A BETTER DAD."

Michael Klim

Father of Stella, Frankie and Rocco

Swimmer / Olympic gold medallist
Owner and founder of Milk & Co Skincare

294

How do you compare the highs
of being a dad with the high of
being an Olympian? You can't.
They're just not in the same
sphere. I was very fortunate
to win Olympic gold and break
world records at the same time.
That was the highest achievement
I could experience in sport.
The adrenaline, the rush, the
adulation from the crowd . . .
it was incredible.

Michael Klim

But the highs of parenthood are more intimate. That's the thing that I was never prepared for as a dad: those insatiable emotions of love and appreciation and pride. In sport, when you win, it's almost like a feeling of relief. You work towards something and obviously you're proud of your achievements, but it's not such a nurturing emotion. The highs of being an Olympian are momentary, but the highs of being a dad are ongoing.

The one thing nobody told me about fatherhood was how challenging it is. It can be bloody hard at times. But it's also incredibly rewarding.

Right now actually feels like the hardest phase of fatherhood so far. Like quite a few dads out there, I've gone through some changing personal circumstances as well as a divorce. That's required a lot of adaptation both for the kids and myself.

Through all that, my priority has just been to try and be the best dad that I can be for the kids. It's been a difficult period for me personally, but I've just tried to ensure that the kids are okay and keep them as unaffected as possible during what could be an unsettling time.

My support network—my partner, friends and family—has been really, really important in helping me get through the tough times. Self-care is a big factor, too. I still try to look after myself because my fitness and swimming help me mentally cope with stress. But I've also worked on the emotional side of things. Mindfulness is something that I've focused on by making more time to stop and reflect. I'm attempting to declutter my life by trying to say no a lot more. There were probably times in the past where I was trying to do too much. But I'm now focused on creating a more sustainable lifestyle so I can spend as much time as possible with the kids.

Divorce has, I feel, made me a better dad. It has made me prioritise what is important to me, and the kids are very important. Their happiness is very important.

TFH

What part of my dad game am
I working on at the moment?
Well, I'm definitely working on my
jump shot, I haven't won a game
of horse against Rocco for about
two years and he's only ten. I need
to get better at Connect 4 against
Frankie, too. She's a genius at that.

But I'm also working on being
my kids' friend as well as their
parent. As a dad, you have to
be authoritarian at times, but
you've also got to have fun.
Sometimes I get too carried away
making sure the structure is there
for my kids and they're doing the
right thing. But ultimately, what
makes me the happiest is when
the kids are having fun. So I'm
working on having more fun
with them myself.

The best piece of advice I've ever
been given about parenting is to
be adaptable, because there's no
manual. We're dealing with these
human beings that are a compilation
of different DNA, and they're their
own individual beings.
Sometimes as a dad, you can be
convinced that you're doing the right
thing. But you have to remember
that your kids have a voice, too; it's
really important to listen to them.

I think you also have to help
your kids overcome their fears.
For example, my son, Rocco, was
really nervous before his school
swimming carnival. There was all
this expectation on him due to
having a father that was a swimmer,
and he was worried about that
judgement from his peers. Rocco
didn't want to swim. But I gently
encouraged him and made sure that
he was signed up for every event.

Michael Klim

At first, he was a little embarrassed about getting up there on the blocks, but he managed to overcome those emotions. In the last event of the day, Rocco swam past one of his schoolmates to win the breaststroke. To this day, he always remembers that moment.

For him to have such a positive experience after I nudged him out of his comfort zone was pretty rewarding. Sometimes, the greatest rewards come from the greatest challenges and a lot of growth can happens in those periods. I felt super-proud of Rocco for the way that he managed to face down his fears.

"What part of my dad game am I working on at the moment? Well, I'm definitely working on my jump shot, I haven't won a game of horse against Rocco for about two years."

You don't have to be
an instruction manual.
You just have to be there.

"BEING A FIGHTER HAS DEFINITELY HELPED ME AS A MAN AND AS A FATHER."

Robert Whittaker

Father of Jack, John and Lilliana

UFC World Middleweight Champion

TFH

When I walk into the octagon, I always tap my chest. People often see that as me tapping my Southern Cross tattoo, and I don't mind it being interpreted like that because I am very proud of my country. But there's another reason why I do it: my father got me that tattoo when I was eighteen. And whether he's in the crowd or in the stands or at home, it's a way for him to know that I'm thinking of him. It's my way of showing him that I know he's watching.

My father was always very supportive. For a while when we first moved in with him as little kids, he looked after us full-time on his own. He was a great dad; he was always present. He made sure there was food on the table, he cooked for us, he did all our washing and he cleaned the house. He did it all.

When I was a kid I didn't understand how tough that would have been. I was a little shit, to be honest. But looking back, I can see that my father sacrificed a lot. He did a lot of things I'm sure he didn't want to do, and he always put us first. So I have a lot of respect for him and I also take inspiration from how he was.

My father proved that you can still be a great dad if you're doing it on your own. Whatever your situation, you just need to be the best parent you can be. There's no single definitive path, it's just about trying to do your best.

Dad was strict when he needed to be, but supportive. He always made sure me and my brother played sports so that we'd stay out of mischief. He enrolled us both into karate school when I was six. That was all about self-defence. Dad did tae kwon do when he was younger, and he was in the army too, so he could see the value in self-defence.

> **"How would I feel if one of my sons wanted to be a UFC fighter? Mate, it would crush me. It would!"**

Being a fighter has definitely helped me as a man and as a father. I've had to do a lot of soul-searching on my journey to become a martial artist. There is nothing more exposing and humbling than getting your arse handed to you, or having a bad day in the gym when you're expected to be at the top of your game. But it's things like that that make you aware of what's really important in life.

Robert Whittaker

A lot of fighters get very swept up in the limelight and they start to change who they are. Whereas I know who I am and I know what counts. There's nothing better than coming home after a hard day and seeing my kids' little smiles.

What's been my proudest moment as a dad? I'm still at that stage where my kids do anything and I'm so proud. My son toilet-trained himself and I was stoked! I get so swept up in everything they do.

The biggest thing that having kids has taught me as a fighter is that I'm really nothing special. When I came home with the world-champ belt, my son just looked at me and dragged me to his LEGO set. He didn't care about the belt, he didn't care about the fight, he just wanted me to play LEGO. That's humbling in the sense that it makes you realise there are lots of people out there that don't like watching fights, and they don't care either—you're a nobody to them. It makes you wake up a bit.

How I am in the octagon is completely separate from how I am as a father and as a loving husband at home. At home, that's who I really am. The other persona is a job. I understand that when I step into the octagon, I'm walking into the office.

I'm there for a purpose and when the job is done, I leave it there and I go back to being a father and a husband. I used to travel for my fight camps and go to Canada to train, but the travelling and the time away from my wife and my father and mother just became too much. It started to affect me emotionally and have a direct effect on my training, so I stopped. And that was before I had kids, so the idea of doing that now is just preposterous.

If I had to sacrifice my time with my family to be the world champ then being the world champ just wouldn't be worth it. When it comes to pushing me forward, there's nothing stronger—nothing more powerful—than my family. My family gives me direction and also gives me fulfilment. They are what makes everything worth doing.

How would I feel if one of my sons wanted to be a UFC fighter? Mate, it would crush me. It would! I'm very emotional with my family. When one of my boys hurts himself, I go into meltdown mode; I want to try and destroy whatever they scraped their knee on! But the thing is, I also know that they're going to do whatever they want to do. The best thing that I can do for them as a father is to make sure they have the right skill set to do whatever they want to do.

TFH

Research shows that father
involvement is linked to greater
maternal satisfaction and lower
rates of maternal depression.
And, crucially, positive father
engagement is associated
with higher educational achievement
and higher self-esteem, especially
among girls, and lower levels
of machismo among boys.

"WE MADE THE DECISION TO BE PRESENT, HANDS-ON PARENTS WHILE TRYING TO KEEP THAT CREATIVE SIDE OF OURSELVES SATISFIED, TOO."

Damian Lewis

Father of Manon and Gulliver

Actor

INTERVIEW BY
Jenny Cooney / HFPA

I know people who have put
their careers to one side
almost entirely for five, six,
seven years while they bring
their kids up. Some of them
get lucky, and they can get
right back on the horse and
just keep going. Others are
less lucky. They find that
there isn't as interesting work
for them when they come
back because they just sat
out for too long.

Damian Lewis

I think both Helen and I made the decision that—as best we could—we'd be present, hands-on parents while trying to keep that creative side of ourselves satisfied, too. We'd keep working and not only stay creatively satisfied, but also not derail our entire careers.

You don't want to be the person that goes, 'I'm just going to look after my kids for six or seven years,' and then find no-one wants to work with you afterwards. Because you do still need to make money, so it is a difficult decision for any parent.

It's also a really difficult decision when a lot of your work is away from home. You know, we're gypsies. We've moved the whole family to LA but then there's work in Toronto, London and Vancouver. It's hard. We all muddle through somehow.

"We all muddle through somehow."

THE OTHER NIGHT

The other night when I was holding you tight,
you said, 'Thank you for making me, me.'
But who made who? And one question for thee:
Am I holding you, or are you holding me?

WILD HORSES

The most powerful story I've ever
heard about fatherhood.

Darrell Brown

Father of Cody and Taylor

Cinematographer / Author of *One Father's Journey to Raise Confident,
Connected, Compassionate Boys*

About ten years ago,
I got to work for a couple
of days with Monty Roberts.
That name might not mean
anything to a lot of people,
but Monty is probably
better known as 'the Horse
Whisperer'. He's the guy
Robert Redford played
in the film.

Monty is in his eighties now. But at the time I met him, he was travelling all over the world doing 300 shows a year. How it worked was that his team would call ahead to equestrian centres in the cities where Monty was about to do an event. Monty got them to find people who owned horses that were the worst of the worst. He wanted the horses that you couldn't put a saddle on, that you couldn't ride, that you couldn't do anything with. Those were the horses that he would work with at the event.

My assignment was to film this short doco with Monty. I remember the first day I got introduced to him, we were chatting for a while and he said to me, 'You got any kids?' I told him I had two little boys who were both toddlers. Monty looked at me and said, 'Well, they're a little bit like wild horses, aren't they?'

What happened over the next two days was fascinating. One woman brought her horse into the auditorium and she said, 'This horse won't go into its float, so for me to take it anywhere, it takes about three hours. I usually need two or three big men to get it on the float.'

Monty said, 'Well, what if I said that in about an hour from now that horse will walk into that float by itself?'

'Well, that will be some sort of a miracle if you did that,' the woman said.

Then Monty said to the owner: 'Tell me everything you know about this horse. I want to know his background, how he was treated, what he was like when he was younger. Tell me about what he will do and tell me about what he won't do.'

'Raising horses is a lot like raising children. Our kids are born with wild spirit, with adventure. Our job isn't to break that spirit. Our job is to communicate with it.'

At first, Monty just looked at this horse and walked around it. He spoke to the horse but didn't approach it. He told the audience what he thought the horse was doing and thinking. He observed the horse's patterns of behaviour. Then he said, 'You'll have noticed that I haven't gone over to the horse yet, I haven't touched the horse at all. That's because the horse hasn't invited me into that space yet. You've got to wait for that sacred moment when that horse invites you in.'

He kept on talking. Then he'd walk close to the horse and the horse would move away.

But Monty just took his time and eventually when he got up close, he explained, 'You wait for this moment now when the horse's ears will just drop back.' Then he puts his hand up and the horse touched his hand with its nose.

'That's the moment we call "join up",' Monty said. 'Join-up is that moment when the horse invites you into its space. Until you have that relationship, nothing will work with the horse but force. Until then, that's the only thing that will get the horse to obey.

'Getting to join up might take a while with some horses,' he said. 'But I just have to sit back, read the horse, observe it and communicate with it until I get to that place.'

Then Monty did this thing where he would sort of lead the horse towards the float and then push it back two steps and say, 'No, you're not going in there.' Then he'd bring the horse towards the float again and push it back again. It was like he was doing this kind of reverse psychology with the horse. Eventually, he led the horse all the way up on the float and pushed it all the way back down again.

Finally, he said to the woman, 'Are you ready to watch your horse walk onto his float?' He turned his back on the horse and stood there, and the horse just came up and nudged him in the back and he walked all the way up the ramp into the float and the horse just walked in with him.

Monty said to the woman, 'You will never have to worry about floating this horse again. From now on, he will just walk straight in.'

Over the next two days I saw Monty work with all kinds of horses. He worked with a horse that was terrified of plastic, but Monty built a relationship with it until he could put a tarpaulin on its back. I saw him work with a horse that would never take a saddle, but Monty managed to put a saddle on it and ride the horse within half an hour. He did all these amazing things. There was not a single horse that he could not work out how to communicate with.

On the very last day, Monty walked into the middle of the auditorium, put down a chair and spoke to the crowd.

'It was my dad that taught me about horses,' he said. 'When I was a young lad, my dad had a big ranch. Owners around the land would bring us their wild horses and I used to watch my dad and his trainers whip and beat these horses. Finally, through force and aggression, they would break their spirit. They would put a saddle on them and they would give them back to the owners as a broken horse that was ready to obey and do whatever they wanted.

'Deep down, I always thought that wasn't the best way to communicate with a horse. So I started working with horses on my own away from the ranch. And I found a way of communicating with horses that was a lot more effective—like I've shown you over this weekend.

'One day when I was seventeen, I said to my dad, "I think I've found a way of getting horses to comply and to do what you want in a fraction of the time without all the men and all the aggression."

'My dad looked at me and said, "No, don't be stupid. This is the way it's done and this is the way it'll always be done".'

Monty said it wasn't long after that that his father died. He never got to see the way that Monty was able to communicate with horses in a way that was completely different, using compassion, patience and understanding.

Monty said: 'The interesting thing is my dad raised his children the same way he raised his horses. My dad used a lot of aggression, he used to hit us, he used to force us to comply.'

That was just the way his father was taught, he explained. Back then, a lot of men raised their kids that way. 'You got to understand a lot of these men came through a war, they came through some pretty tough times,' Monty said. 'In order to deal with that, they shut themselves off emotionally. What they did know was that you could get people to do things by using force.'

Monty said, 'If you understand what I've done with horses, you'll understand that raising horses is a lot like raising children. Our kids are born with wild spirit, with adventure. Our job isn't to break that spirit. Our job is to communicate with it.'

As Monty was telling this story, I was looking around the auditorium and there were people with tears just running down their face. They knew that what Monty was saying was so right and so important.

Monty said: 'We live in a world where, particularly with young boys, we don't understand their wild spirit and their sense of adventure. We don't understand why they don't want to sit still in class. So we try and medicate that out of them. We try and discipline it. But you don't need to do that at all. You just need to communicate with that spirit, you need to talk to it, you need to invite it into the outside world. Boys are meant to run; their life isn't meant to always be in a

"Boys are meant to run. Their life is out there in the forest, in the hills and in the rivers."

The Horse Whisperer

book or a classroom. Their life is out there in the forest, in the hills and in the rivers. With boys, you need to let them run. They're born to be risk takers. Your job is to guide that and speak to that and communicate with that. You need to watch it and try and understand it.

'Just like with the horse, you got to be invited in. You've got to look for certain patterns and try and find a way in. Parenting is a dance, and being a father is the best personal development course you'll ever do. It's about you learning how to find ways to communicate with their spirit and guide it and bring love to the experience.'

Monty's story was so powerful for everyone in the room. It was just this beautiful metaphor for raising your own children—that to get them to follow you into the float, you didn't have to do it by force. You could do it by modelling values to them, by modelling integrity, by modelling what healthy masculinity looks like, by modelling what patience looks like. You can tell your kids what you want. But if you model those things in their vicinity, then they'll become who you are.

"Being a father is the best personal development course you'll ever do.'

I never forgot that story. My sons were about three and four at the time and that story just spoke directly to my soul. My wife, Jules, and I used to love our boys' spirits and their sense of adventure. We thrived on it. Our sons gave us an energy that we had lost ourselves.

As parents, you learn to act appropriately in the adult world, and we do lose that sense of adventure and risk-taking and playfulness that we all need. I think if we actually managed to hold onto that, we'd become better entrepreneurs, better adventurers. But we'd also have a lot more fun in our own lives, too.

MEET THE MEN BEHIND THE FATHER HOOD

Luke Benedictus

Father of Joe and Marc

Luke has spent 20 years working as a writer and editor across
an assortment of magazines, newspapers and websites. Before jumping
ship to help launch the-father-hood.com, he was the editor of the
Australian edition of *Men's Health*. Former lives include working as editor
of *Dazed & Confused* (Australia) and stints at *The Age*, *The Sunday Age*,
The Sun Online (UK) and *Eurosport* (France). Having grown up in England,
Luke moved to Australia in 2002 and now lives in Sydney with his wife,
Sarah, and two young sons. He was compelled to have children primarily
as an outlet for his weak puns and feeble one-liners.

Jeremy Macvean

Father of Amara, Nellie and Violet

Jeremy breathed a sigh of relief when the teacher of his male-only antenatal class shared the following advice: 'To be a good dad, turn up and try.' So that's what Jeremy's been doing ever since: turning up to invest time and emotional energy into himself and his marriage with Emily; turning up to the birth of his three girls, without fainting; turning up to family holidays (despite them not being the slightest bit relaxing); turning up to build tribes of healthier, happier men through his work at Movember Foundation. Through his business, Radiate, he's also turning up to share two decades' worth of experience in the areas of marketing, digital brand building and health promotion with the likes of Southern Cross Austereo, Peter Mac, The Women's Hospital and Sensis. Of every role Jeremy has ever played, fatherhood brings him by far the most joy, and is also by far the most challenging.

Andrew McUtchen

Father of Indie, Isla and Neve, and friend of stepdaughter, Alyssa

First, Andrew was a journalist, writing for *GQ* for five years as an Associate Editor as well as *The Age* and *QANTAS*. Then he was a publisher, founding Story Matters Most, which won a Gourmand World Cookbook Award for *Chin Chin: The Book*. Most recently, he became an entrepreneur, founding *Time+Tide*, which is among the world's most-read wristwatch websites and the official watch partner of *WISH Magazine* in *The Australian*. Somewhere in the midst of all that, he and his wife, Fiona, had three daughters in four years. Now, he intends to combine everything—writing, publishing, building a digital tribe and madly scrambling to raise his children with love and attention—in The Father Hood, Australia's new online destination for fathers.

NOTES

Words from the wise

p. 41   **'Any fool can have a child . . .'**, Barack Obama, Father's Day speech
             at Apostolic Church of God in Chicago, Illinois, June 15, 2008

p. 41   **'I'll be thinking about whether I did right by all of them . . .'**, Barack Obama;
             Morehouse College commencement address in Atlanta, Georgia, May 19, 2013

p. 73   **'When you are childless . . .'**, Will Self, 'A Point of View: Can parents
             and non-parents ever understand each other?'; *BBC Magazine*,
             <www.bbc.com/news/magazine-31149081>, 2015, accessed March 23, 2019

p. 103   **'Children don't grow up. They disappear.'**, Maxine Ventham (Author),
             Shelagh Milligan (Foreword), *Spike Milligan: His Part in Our Lives*,
             Anova Books, 2002

p. 129   **'Any idiot can face a crisis . . .'**, Anton Chekov

p. 149   **'For unflagging interest and enjoyment . . .'**, Theodore Roosevelt

p. 199   **'One of the greatest things a father can do . . .'**, Howard W. Hunter,
             'Being a Righteous Father and Husband', <www.lds.org/general
             conference/1994/10/being-a-righteous-husband-and-father?lang=eng>,
             accessed April 24, 2019

p. 217   **'Raising children is terribly hard work . . .'**, Andrew Solomon, *Far From
             the Tree: Parents, Children and the Search for Identity*, Scribner, 2012

p. 235   **'Both parents have known someone . . .'**, Graham Greene, *A Sort of Life*,
             The Bodley Head, 1971

p. 255   **'At sixteen . . .'**, Salman Rushdie, *East, West*, Vintage, 1998

p. 285   **'Children have never been very good at listening to their elders . . .'**,
             James Baldwin, 'Fifth Avenue, Uptown', *Esquire*,, 1960, accessed March 31, 2019

Dad stats

pp. 27, 237 & 243 Emma Dodds, 'You'll NEVER guess how many nappies you'll change before your child turns four', <https://closeronline.co.uk/real-life/news how-many-nappies-change-baby/>, 2018, accessed April 20, 2019

pp. 64–7 Dr Laura King, 'Supporting Active Fatherhood in Britain', History & Policy, <www.historyandpolicy.org/policy-papers/papers/supporting-active fatherhood-in-britain>, 2012, accessed April 29, 2019

P. 95 The Child and Family Research Partnership at the LBJ School of Public Affairs at The University of Texas at Austin, 'Infographic: The Importance of Father Involvement', < https://childandfamilyresearch.utexas.edu/ news/infographic-importance-father-involvement>, June 2015, accessed May 16, 2019

pp. 75, 186 & 214 Hall & Partners and Open Mind, 'Healthy Dads? The challenge of being a new father (A summary prepared for Beyond Blue)', August 2015, <www.beyondblue.org.au/docs/default-source/research-project-files bw0314-beyondblue-healthy-dads-summary.pdf?sfvrsn=610243ea _ 0>, accessed April 20, 2019

p. 115 Kim Parker and Gretchen Livingston, '7 Facts about American Dads', Pew Research Center, FactTank: News in the Numbers, <www.pewresearch.org/fact-tank/2018/06/13/fathers-day-facts/>, 2018, accessed April 29, 2019

pp. 144–5 Gretchen Livingston, 'Growing Number of Dads Home with the Kids', Pew Research Center, <www.pewsocialtrends.org/2014/06/05 growing-number-of-dads-home-with-the-kids/>, 2014, accessed April 29, 2019

p. 160 Natalie Yeo, 'The New and Improved Aussie Dad: Fashionable, financially secure and family-oriented', Nielsen, <https://www.nielsen.com/nz/en insights/news/2017/the-new-and-improved-aussie-dad-fashionable financially-secure-and-family-oriented.print.html>, 2017, accessed April 20, 2019

p. 249 McCrindle, '50 Surprising Statistics about Australia', McCrindle, <https://mccrindle.com.au/insights/blogarchive/50-surprising-statistics-about-australia/>, accessed March 20, 2019

p. 283 Zero To Three, 'National Parent Survey Report', <www.zerotothree.org resources/1425-national-parent-survey-report>, 2016, accessed April 20, 2019

p. 307 Tawanda Makusha and Linda M. Richter, 'Fathers need to get involved in the first 1000 days of their kids' lives', The Conversation, <https:// theconversation.com/fathers-need-to-get-involved-in-the-first-1000-days -of-their-kids-lives-100779>, 2018, accessed April 20, 2019

TFH

Andrew, Luke and Jeremy
would like to thank:

None of this would have happened without our partners, our wives, our co-pilots: Fiona, Sarah and Emily. Thank you for making us dads.

Yes, there were times, I'm sure you knew,
When I bit off more than I could chew.
But through it all, when there was doubt,
I ate it up and spit it out.
I faced it all and I stood tall . . .
I dad it my way. – With apologies to Frank Sinatra

We're all working this out as we go along, and our nine kids/stepkids often bear the brunt of this. Thanks to Indie, Isla, Neve, Alyssa, Joe, Marc, Amara, Nellie, and Violet for being on this endless bear hunt with us—we're not sure who is growing more.

Grandparents really are the saviours of modern family life *(our kids are big fans of theirs)*. Special thanks to Mela, Jenny, Rob, Allen, Jane, Tanya, David, Lyn, Rhonda and Greg for all your help in making our lives slightly less demented.

Standing behind the three of us is a band of brothers *(literally)*. Thanks to Pete, Chris, Phil, Dan, Tony and Fraser, the siblings who continue to be the wingmen in our lives.

The Father Hood would also like to thank

Ron Barnacle, Steve Biddulph, Wayne Bradshaw, Katie Bosher, Darrell Brown, Chief Brabon, Emilie Brabon, Joe Brumm, Tim Cahill, Amy Carroll, Jenny Cooney, Harold David, Michael Da Gama Pinto, Titus Day, Ben Dillon-Smith, Thomas Docking, Kelly Doust, Nicki Ferguson, Emily Kawalilak, Professor Richard Fletcher, Nick Fordham, Osher Günsberg, Tom Harkin, Scott Henderson, Aladdin Jones, Amir Kefkovic, Jeesoo Kim, Madonna King, Michael Klim, Alex Laguna, Adam MacDougall, Peter Maddison, Tim Meyer, Sam Moor, Grainne O'Loughlin, Donte Palmer, Megan Pigott, Jonni Pollard, Nicholas Pollock, Professor Paul Ramchandani, Professor Bruce Robinson, Pete Rhodes, Dylan Roos, Paul Roos, Nick Thorn, Paul Villanti, Emma Walsh, Carol Warwick, Tristan White, Rob Whittaker, Steve Willis, Justin Wolfers and Gus Worland.

Acknowledgements

JOIN THE MOVEMENT

**Navigating dads to their best lives.
Since right now.**

f   @the.father.hood.home

⊙   @the-father.hood

in   @the-father-hood

▶   @thefatherhood

www.the-father-hood.com

Just keep turning up.